Barnes & Noble Shakespeare

David Scott Kastan
Series Editor

BARNES & NOBLE SHAKESPEARE features newly edited texts of the plays prepared by the world's premiere Shakespeare scholars. Each edition provides new scholarship with an introduction, commentary, unusually full and informative notes, an account of the play as it would have been performed in Shakespeare's theaters, and an essay on how to read Shakespeare's language.

DAVID SCOTT KASTAN is the Old Dominion Foundation Professor in the Humanities at Columbia University and one of the world's leading authorities on Shakespeare.

Barnes & Noble Shakespeare
Published by Barnes & Noble
122 Fifth Avenue
New York, NY 10011
www.barnesandnoble.com/shakespeare

Image on p. 304:
By Permission of the Folger Shakespeare Library.

Library of Congress Cataloging-in-Publication Data

Shakespeare, William, 1564–1616.
Much ado about nothing / William Shakespeare.
p. cm.
Includes bibliographical references.
ISBN-13: 978-1-4114-0055-9
ISBN-10: 1-4114-0055-0
1. Courtship—Drama. 2. Conspiracies—Drama. 3. Messina (Italy)—Drama. 4. Rejection (Psychology)—Drama. I. Title.

PR2828.A1 2006
822.3'3—dc22

2006018841

Printed and bound in the United States.

5 7 9 10 8 6

MUCH ADO ABOUT NOTHING

William SHAKESPEARE

ROBERT S. MIOLA
EDITOR

Barnes & Noble Shakespeare

Contents

Introduction to *Much Ado About Nothing*

by Robert S. Miola

One of Shakespeare's sparkling comedies, *Much Ado About Nothing* perplexes audiences even as it delights them. Benedick and Beatrice insult and mock each other. Are they former or present lovers? Claudio courts Hero, gives her up for lost, courts her again, rejects her for supposed infidelity, repents (after a fashion), and finally weds her. Is this love or confusion?

Such questions prove the truth of the title, *Much Ado About Nothing*, especially when we remember that "nothing" (pronounced "noting" in Elizabethan English) means also "observing." Audiences and readers—by nature noters all—watch the play and try to make sense of the witty characters and dazzling action. Our confusions mirror those of the people on stage, who observe, consider, question, and draw conclusions (sometimes wrong). For them as for the audiences, the play insistently calls into question the business of noting, that is, our human capacity to perceive and make sense of the world.

Take for example the observations and confusions of the masquerade scene (2.1), that delightful and dizzying musical interlude. In an episode absent from the sources of the play, the men (Leonato, Benedick, Claudio, and perhaps the villain Don John) mistakenly believe that Don Pedro courts Hero for himself, not for his friend Claudio. As unmasked women and masked men pair off for witty banter and dance, they enact in miniature the couplings and uncouplings, the posings and exposings, the perceptions and deceptions that constitute love and courtship in this play. But the masked men cannot fool the women. Ursula recognizes old Antonio by his waggling head and dry hand; Beatrice recognizes Benedick and mocks him mercilessly. As she said earlier, merrily railing against marriage: "I have a good eye, uncle; I can see a church by daylight" (2.1.71). In the business of noting, the women in this scene and in the play see more clearly than the men.

Women and men, women against men. The eternal competition drives the play as the opposing sexes struggle for love, happiness, marriage, money, and *maistrye* ("power"), as Chaucer's Wife of Bath put it. Why else would Shakespeare add to the source stories the merry war between Beatrice and Benedick? The verbal fireworks and sexual energy of these two have commanded the stage since the first performances. And the actors who have played the roles appear through the centuries as famous duets: David Garrick and Hannah Pritchard, Charles and Ellen Kean, Henry Irving and Ellen Terry, John Gielgud and Peggy Ashcroft, Donald Sinden and Judi Dench, Derek Jacobi and Sinead Cusack, Kenneth Branagh and Emma Thompson. These pairs have inflected the age-old struggle with the fears, desires, and values of their particular cultural moments: Garrick and Pritchard (1748–1756) emphasized mirth and wit; Irving and Terry (1882–1895), the underlying goodness and refinement of the pair; Sinden and Dench (1976–1977), the problems of gender roles. Beatrice and Benedick have lived on in numerous theatrical adaptations, sequels, and spin-offs. They serve as prototypes for the witty, sparring lovers in Restoration comedy and in some plays of George Bernard Shaw and Oscar Wilde. They have also inspired a comic opera *Béatrice et Bénédict* (1862) by Hector Berlioz.

It is natural to see the lively Benedick and Beatrice as contrasts to the more conventional lovers Claudio and Hero. But actors and audiences have found surprising similarities in the female opposites, delighting to discover a little Hero in Beatrice and a little Beatrice in Hero. Like Hero, Beatrice suffers from betrayal, recalling a previous relationship with Benedick: "he lent it [his heart] me awhile, and I gave him use for it: a double heart for a single one. Marry, once before he won it of me with false dice" (2.1.248–250; cf. 1.1.126). In Act Three, scene four, she appears vulnerable and overmatched by the suddenly witty Margaret. Later Beatrice obeys unquestioningly the social code that relegates revenge exclusively to men.

Hero, on the other hand, is not simply Goody Two-Shoes, the silent, romantic, obedient daughter, as she has been too frequently and simplistically portrayed. Hero understands perfectly the masculine codes that govern love and life in Messina, but she stubbornly insists on the rebato ("collar") of her choice before the wedding (3.4.6). And she parodies the clever Beatrice with perfect pitch and venom, professing the wit and apprehension some have found lacking in her:

> I never yet saw man,
> How wise, how noble, young, how rarely featured
> But she would spell him backward. If fair-faced,
> She would swear the gentleman should be her sister;
> If black, why, nature, drawing of an antic,
> Made a foul blot; if tall, a lance ill-headed;
> If low, an agate very vilely cut;
> If speaking, why, a vane blown with all winds;
> If silent, why, a block movèd with none.
> So turns she every man the wrong side out
> And never gives to truth and virtue that
> Which simpleness and merit purchaseth. (3.1.59–70)

Shakespeare rarely settles for simple contrasts; as Beatrice and Hero illustrate, people are complicated and surprising.

Hero's parody of Beatrice, of course, appears as part of a plot to get Beatrice and Benedick together. Knowing that Beatrice is eavesdropping, Hero and her friends talk loudly of Benedick's secret love for her. Beatrice comes to a serious and sober realization:

> What fire is in mine ears? Can this be true?
> Stand I condemned for pride and scorn so much?
> Contempt, farewell, and maiden pride, adieu!
> No glory lives behind the back of such.
> And Benedick, love on; I will requite thee,
> Taming my wild heart to thy loving hand.
> If thou dost love, my kindness shall incite thee
> To bind our loves up in a holy band. (3.1.107–114)

Beatrice for the first time in the play speaks in verse not prose, and in rhymed lines at that. Taking an honest look at herself and her famous wit, she surrenders to a hidden desire for love and marriage.

This scene follows the parallel eavesdropping of Benedick on his friends, who loudly talk of Beatrice's secret love for him. Shakespeare takes pains to differentiate these two scenes, contrasting Beatrice's serious moment of revelation with Benedick's comic self-discovery. Benedick always gets laughs when he makes his grand resolution: "I will be horribly in love with her" (2.3.219). He changes his long-held position against love with the mock-altruistic declaration, "The world must be peopled" (2.3.226). In the joyful 1993 film version of the play, Kenneth Branagh and company well play the comedy of the first eavesdropping. At first hearing of Beatrice's love, the shocked Benedick collapses his chair and falls flat on his rear end; he covers an involuntary exclamation of protest with an improvised bird call, "Caw, Caw, Caw." Branagh's Benedick airily dismisses his former railing against love with a wave of the hand, "doth not the appetite alter" (2.3.222).

Into the tangle of self-generated deceptions in the play Shakespeare introduces an external agent of confusion—the villain Don John. Don John tries to ruin the upcoming marriage of Claudio and Hero by making Claudio believe that Hero is cheating on him. Don John succinctly summarizes himself in the beginning ("I am a plain-dealing villain" 1.3.27–28) and stays in character to the end. (I once saw an interesting attempt at a psychological reading by an Oxford student who played the part with a pronounced stutter. But such a mannerism can only go so far.) The speech prefixes and stage directions in the Quarto identify Don John as a bastard, the illegitimate brother of Don Pedro, in other words, as an outsider, a malcontent. Don John has "of late stood out against" (1.3.17–18) Don Pedro in the war, suffered defeat, and now been "reconciled" (1.1.135) to his brother. Sullen and angry, and jealous, he resents Claudio. "That young start-up hath all the glory of my overthrow" (1.3.56–57). Still, a large part of his malice seems gratuitous and his character remains something of a mystery. In all versions of the source story the villain is a jealous, unsuccessful suitor but Shakespeare strips this motivation away. The Don John character in Shakespeare's principal source, Bandello's *Novelle* (1554), repents, confesses, receives forgiveness, and shares in the final wedding scene with a new bride; Shakespeare's Don John simply disappears and is captured off stage.

The great Romantic poet and critic Samuel Taylor Coleridge rightly noted the curiously flat portrayal of Don John, "the mainspring of the plot," but undeveloped by the playwright, simply "shown and withdrawn." [1] And yet, Don John has not simply wandered into the wrong play from some Elizabethan melodrama. He takes his name from the historical Don John of Austria (1547–1578), bastard half brother to Philip II of Spain. Don John defeated the Turks at Lepanto and dreamed of invading England to restore Roman Catholicism to the land. Living on in the Elizabethan imagination, the name Don John

1. *Shakespearean Criticism*, ed. Thomas Middleton Raysor, 2 vols. (New York: Dutton, 1961–1962), 1: 200.

makes the fictional character a potent and menacing presence in the play, here tamed and rendered harmless by the plot of the comedy.

Don John, moreover, belongs to a great Shakespearean tradition of opposing brothers, beginning with the identical twins in *The Comedy of Errors*, extending through the fraternal battles in the history plays, the fratricidal struggles in the tragedies (Claudius and Elder Hamlet, Edmund, also illegitimate, and Edgar in *King Lear*), and concluding in the conflicts between Alonso and Sebastian, and Prospero and Antonio in *The Tempest*. Don John is the tragic plotter and loner; Don Pedro, the comic plotter and would-be Cupid who seeks to bring together Claudio and Hero, Benedick and Beatrice.

The apparent opposition between these two brothers, like that between Hero and Beatrice, conceals some similarities. Don Pedro, too, is named after a historical character, Don Pedro of Aragon (Peter III of Aragon, 1239–1285), who came to power in Sicily after the Sicilian Vespers (March 30, 1282), a massacre of Sicilians, including pregnant women, judged sympathetic to the French rulers. The Sicilians accepted the leadership of Peter III, and fought battles under him against the expelled French for several decades, one of which, presumably, constitutes the "action" (1.1.5) that immediately precedes the play. Don Pedro, the real ruler of Sicily, first offers to "break" (1.1.289) or reveal the news of Claudio's love, then, surprisingly, offers to woo Hero in his place:

> I will assume thy part in some disguise
> And tell fair Hero I am Claudio,
> And in her bosom I'll unclasp my heart
> And take her hearing prisoner with the force
> And strong encounter of my amorous tale. (1.1.284–288)

Don Pedro never explains why he chooses to impersonate Claudio rather than simply act as love broker; and he describes his planned wooing in an unsavory mix of sexual and military imagery that recalls his historical namesake's violent rise to power. Without warning, he suddenly offers Beatrice a proposal that may be comic or serious on stage: "Will you have me, lady?" (2.1.292). In either case the potentially arrogant assertion of self manifest in such actions echoes in Don Pedro's aspiration to replace Cupid and, with his accomplices, become the "only love gods" (2.1.344–345). Don Pedro falls for his brother's trick and participates fully in the rejection of Hero, whom he coldly refers to as "The old man's daughter" (5.1.172–173). Ironically, the master plotter and new love god, Benedick notes, is left unmatched in the end. "Prince, thou art sad. Get thee a wife; get thee a wife" (5.4.122–123). Don Pedro is no Don John, of course, but he may come across as a powerful and disturbing meddler.

And what of his brother's plot against Hero and Claudio? Don John has his friend Borachio enter Hero's house and address Margaret who, in some fashion, impersonates Hero and completely fools Claudio and Don Pedro, spying and noting and misperceiving everything. But Don John's plot creaks frequently and noisily. How does a lowlife like Borachio contrive to make Hero, the governor's daughter, absent from her bedroom the night before her wedding (2.2.39–41)? How does he persuade Margaret to enact such a ridiculous and demeaning charade, and why does she, so clever elsewhere, never put two and two together to save her mistress and the day? Why doesn't Claudio ever ask Hero what is going on? Furthermore, as Lewis Carroll jestingly complained to the famous Beatrice, Ellen Terry, why doesn't Hero simply tell Claudio the truth: "Well, then, granting that Hero slept in some other room that night, why didn't she say so? When Claudio asks her, 'What man was he talked with you yesternight / Out at your window betwixt twelve and one?' why doesn't she reply, "I talked with no man at that hour, my lord: / Nor was I in my chamber yesternight, / But in another, far from it remote.'"[2]

2. *Much Ado About Nothing*, ed. F. H. Mares (Cambridge: Cambridge Univ. Press, 2003), 169.

To be sure, slanderers generally get their way on the Elizabethan stage, and these villains take care to arrange the ocular proof a similar Shakespearean dupe, Othello, demands. But there is more going on here than stage conventions and cheap tricks. In this play as in Shakespeare's *Othello, The Winter's Tale,* and *Cymbeline,* Don John's plot taps into a deep cultural anxiety, the male fear of cuckoldry, of female infidelity. The fear surfaces throughout the play, beginning with the opening jokes about Hero's legitimacy:

> **Don Pedro:** I think this is your daughter.
> **Leonato:** Her mother hath many times told me so.
> **Benedick:** Were you in doubt, sir, that you asked her?
> **Leonato:** Signior Benedick, no, for then were you a child.
> (1.1.89–93)

Benedick rails against marriage and the inevitable cuckold's horns it brings (1.1.210–212, 229–231), and crudely suggests Claudio's bastardy: "some such strange bull leapt your father's cow" (5.4.49). In the closing moments of the play he urges Don Pedro to marry: "There is no staff more reverend than one tipped with horn" (5.4.123–124).

This male fear of female infidelity drives and effectuates Don John's plot and the entire play. As elsewhere, male desire here is aggressive and possessive; in Elizabethan slang the "nothing" these men make much ado about signifies also "female genitals." Male desire is also potentially violent, allied to militarism; these men are soldiers with a high regard for their own conquests, martial and marital, as well as their own honor. Female chastity functions as a flash point in the explosive setting of Mediterranean, specifically Italian, machismo. The details may not be realistic, but the plot itself and the passions it arouses are real enough.

The practices of both brothers come to a remarkable climax in the wedding scene (4.1), the focal point of almost every production.

Don John's deception culminates in Claudio's self-righteous and cruel humiliation of his bride: "Give not this rotten orange to your friend" (4.1.30), he says, as he returns her to her shocked father. Claudio rails against his bride's "savage sensuality" (4.1.59); Leonato joins in the abuse, at one point wishing his daughter dead; Hero faints. Tragic passion threatens to destroy the high-spirited comedy. "This looks not like a nuptial" (4.1.66), Benedick aptly comments.

After the Friar buys time by pleading for calm and suggesting the pretence of Hero's death, one brother's tragedy of broken nuptials yields to the other's comedy of lovers' meeting. Don Pedro's deception culminates in Beatrice and Benedick's revelation of love. Benedick finally speaks honestly: "I do love nothing in the world so well as you. Is not that strange?" (4.1.264–265). After dancing around a bit, Beatrice surrenders:

> **Beatrice**: Why then, God forgive me.
> **Benedick**: What offense, sweet Beatrice?
> **Beatrice**: You have stayed me in a happy hour. I was about to protest I loved you.
> **Benedick**: And do it with all thy heart.
> **Beatrice**: I love you with so much of my heart that none is left to protest. (4.1.277–283)

Dropping the poses and the defenses, Beatrice and Benedick face each other in vulnerability. Shakespeare renders the moment of hard-won revelation and romance in a prose all the more intimate, honest, and moving for the explosion that occasioned it.

Who but Shakespeare would have put both climaxes, the tragic breaking of the wedding and the comic confession of love, in the same scene? But he is not done yet. Beatrice and Benedick's joy is short lived, shattered in the next breath. She responds to his gallant offer, "Come; bid me do anything for thee," with the chilling command, "Kill Claudio." He refuses, "Ha! Not for the wide world." She answers: "You kill me to deny it. Farewell" (4.1.284–287). The violins stop, the magic suddenly ends. Contrary passions sweep these new lovers back into the hard world of relationships in Messina, into the daily, maddening business of managing strong emotions, conflicting desires, and deep hurts, to "the fury and mire of human veins," as W. B. Yeats put it. Beatrice tries to leave and Benedick finally relents, "Enough; I am engaged" (4.1.323), forced to challenge his friend in order to win his wife.

Kill Claudio. The startling command expresses the outrage of Hero's loyal cousin and her conviction about the slanderous plot against her. But generations of readers and spectators have been more than sympathetic to the request. As a character Claudio has drawn fire from all sides. "He's a *bah-stard*, isn't he?" the actor playing Leonato in ACTER's 1988 tour observed summarily after one performance. Charles Gildon, the first critic to write an extended commentary on all the plays, attacked Claudio more elegantly if less pithily: "Claudio's conduct to the woman he loved [is] highly contrary to the very nature of love—to expose her in so barbarous a manner and with so little concern and struggle, and on such weak grounds without a farther examination into the matter." [3] Claudio takes his place in the line of Shakespearean cads—Proteus (*Two Gentlemen of Verona*), Angelo (*Measure for Measure*), and Bertram (*All's Well That Ends Well*)—who are all rewarded with women they manifestly don't deserve and then (in Samuel Johnson's famous phrase) "dismissed to happiness."

In these youths Shakespeare refashions the New Comedic *adulescens*, "young man," often spineless and dishonorable, a staple for comedy from the Greek Menander (4th century B.C.), through Roman playwrights Plautus and Terence, up through television sitcoms. But as a restless experimenter with received traditions, the playwright is up to something else as well. Shakespeare systematically darkens

3. *Shakespeare: The Critical Heritage*, ed. Brian Vickers, 6 vols. (London: Routledge & Kegan Paul, 1974–1981), 2: 241.

Bandello's genteel Timbreo, Claudio's original: Timbreo courts a woman of lower social class for love; Claudio proposes to the governor's daughter and inquires about her inheritance: "Hath Leonato any son, my lord?" (1.1.257). Timbreo woos Fenicia himself; Claudio uses Don John and barely speaks to Hero; Timbreo breaks off the engagement by messenger; Claudio rejects Hero in the church on their wedding day. After the broken wedding Shakespeare continues to convert Bandello's noble lover into his ignoble Claudio. Timbreo grieves upon hearing of Fenicia's death and begins to doubt the evidence of her infidelity: "Sir Timbreo began to feel great sorrow and a heartstirring such as he would never have thought possible. Nevertheless he did not think himself blameworthy, since he had seen a man climb the ladder and enter the house. But then reflecting more on what he had seen, and his anger having cooled, and reason lending him new vision, he thought to himself that maybe the man who had entered the house might have been doing so for another woman than Fenicia, or even to commit a theft."[4]

Timbreo thus acts in perfect accordance with the Friar's plan for Claudio:

When he shall hear she died upon his words,
Th' idea of her life shall sweetly creep
Into his study of imagination,
And every lovely organ of her life
Shall come apparelled in more precious habit,
More moving, delicate, and full of life,
Into the eye and prospect of his soul
Than when she lived indeed. Then shall he mourn,
If ever love had interest in his liver. (4.1.221–229)

4. *Narrative and Dramatic Sources of Shakespeare*, ed. Geoffrey Bullough, 8 vols. (London: Routledge & Kegan Paul, 1957–1975), 2: 122–123.

Unlike Timbreo and the true lover of the Friar's imagination, Claudio callowly dismisses the grieving Antonio and Leonato, mocking their anger: "We had liked to have had our two noses snapped off with two old men without teeth" (5.1.116–117). Claudio does not mourn for Hero, but instead asks Benedick to cheer him up, to jest away his "high-proof melancholy" (5.1.124). So doing, he shows, according to the Friar's prescription, that love has no interest in his liver. Actors and directors excuse the offenses by emphasizing Claudio's youth (cf. 1.1.11–13). But Shakespeare seems determined to defy conventions, to confound our expectations about happy endings, to complicate the journeys that end in lovers' meetings. And to question the lovers themselves, who may be imperfect, even deeply flawed. As noters who observe and assign fault and make judgments, the spectators experience almost as many conflicting signals and confusions as do the characters.

Enter Constable Dogberry, in his own words, "a householder and, which is more, as pretty a piece of flesh as any is in Messina, and one that knows the law, go to, and a rich fellow enough, go to, and a fellow that hath had losses, and one that hath two gowns and everything handsome about him" (4.2.76–81). Officious and endearing, Dogberry tangles up in malapropism (the mistaking of one word for another) the simplest processes of noting, of observing and reporting rightly. He looks for the most "desartless" (deserving) and "senseless" (sensible) man to be constable (3.3.8, 20). He instructs his men to ignore vagrants and drunkards, and to be wary of contamination by association with criminals: "they that touch pitch will be defiled" (3.3.53–54). "O villain!" he exclaims upon discovering Borachio's role in the plot, "Thou wilt be condemned into everlasting redemption for this" (4.2.50–51). (Dogberry has baffled every scholarly editor who has tried to figure out what word inspires his "tedious" in the assertion to Leonato: "if I were as tedious as a king, I could find it in my heart to bestow it all of your Worship," 3.5.17–19.)

Remarkably, Shakespeare makes this incommunicative constable the "savior of the play," in George Bernard Shaw's phrase.[5] Fully appreciating Dogberry's importance, Shaw objected to one production's cutting of his visit to Leonato (3.5), "an exasperating stupidity . . . made traditional on the London stage ever since Sir Henry Irving [1882] (who will have an extremely unpleasant quarter of an hour if he is unlucky enough to come across the Bard in the heavenly Pantheon) ingeniously discovered that means of reducing Dogberry to a minor part." Dogberry's part, Shaw well knew, is to expose Don John's deception and initiate the processes of reconciliation. Assigning this role to the least capable noter in the play, Shakespeare mocks the wisdoms, so called, of all the clever plotters, practicers, and deceivers. "What your wisdoms could not discover, these shallow fools have brought to light" (5.1.225–227).

The final resolution replays with a difference the earlier masquerade. This time the women wear veils and the men, unlike the women earlier, cannot penetrate the disguises. Despite all their posturing and scheming, they must wait upon the women. "Which is the lady I must seize upon?" (5.4.53), says Claudio; "Which is Beatrice?" (5.4.72), says Benedick. Hero reveals herself to an astonished Claudio, who exclaims "Another Hero!" (5.4.62) and expresses no further remorse, relief, or joy. Our final reaction to him will depend to some degree on the effects of the ritualistic scene of mourning at Leonato's monument (5.3), but we shall never confuse him with Romeo. His final lines (often cut in production) sneeringly predict Benedick's infidelity, "if my cousin do not look exceedingly narrowly to thee" (5.4.116–117).

Here Beatrice and Benedick relapse into their old style of witty banter until Claudio and Hero produce their love sonnets, "our own hands against our hearts" (5.4.93). Since the sonnet is the conventional lyric expression of love that circulated in hundreds of

5. *Shaw on Shakespeare*, ed. Edwin Wilson (London: Cassell, 1962), 147.

sequences by European poets, Beatrice and Benedick, these superbly individualized high fliers, herewith join the throng of lovers who sigh, listen to tabors and pipes, and thrust their necks into yokes. Shakespeare takes Benedick down another peg or two by depicting him as an inept sonneteer, struggling to write his "halting sonnet" (5.4.89) in 5.2, until finally giving up in exasperation, "I was not born under a rhyming planet" (5.2.33–34).

These sonnets validate as much as humiliate, however. They signal the lovers' participation in the grand tradition of Renaissance *amor* originating in the *dolce stil nuovo*, "sweet new style," of Italian Renaissance poets Dante and Petrarch. In *La Vita Nuova* and the *Commedia* Dante sang the immortal praises of another Beatrice, the lady who inspired her pilgrim lover to joy and holiness. It can surely be no accident that the name Beatrice means "she who blesses" and the name Benedick derives from *benedictus*, "he who is blessed." The union of these lovers, finally blessing and blessed, finds affirmation in the music and dance that concludes the play and brings all into a general harmony. Perhaps there has been much ado about something, after all.

Shakespeare and His England

by David Scott Kastan

Shakespeare is a household name, one of those few that don't need a first name to be instantly recognized. His first name was, of course, William, and he (and it, in its Latin form, *Gulielmus*) first came to public notice on April 26, 1564, when his baptism was recorded in the parish church of Stratford-upon-Avon, a small market town about ninety miles northwest of London. It isn't known exactly when he was born, although traditionally his birthday is taken to be April 23rd. It is a convenient date (perhaps too convenient) because that was the date of his death in 1616, as well as the date of St. George's Day, the annual feast day of England's patron saint. It is possible Shakespeare was born on the 23rd; no doubt he was born within a day or two of that date. In a time of high rates of infant mortality, parents would not wait long after a baby's birth for the baptism. Twenty percent of all children would die before their first birthday.

Life in 1564, not just for infants, was conspicuously vulnerable. If one lived to age fifteen, one was likely to live into one's fifties, but probably no more than 60 percent of those born lived past their mid-teens. Whole towns could be ravaged by epidemic disease. In 1563, the year before Shakespeare was born, an outbreak of plague claimed over one third of the population of London. Fire, too, was a constant threat; the thatched roofs of many houses were highly flammable, as well as offering handy nesting places for insects and rats. Serious crop failures in several years of the decade of the 1560s created food shortages, severe enough in many cases to lead to the starvation of the elderly and the infirm, and lowering the resistances of many others so that between 1536 and 1560 influenza claimed over 200,000 lives.

Shakespeare's own family in many ways reflected these unsettling realities. He was one of eight children, two of whom did not survive their first year, one of whom died at age eight; one lived to twenty-seven, while the four surviving siblings died at ages ranging from Edmund's thirty-nine to William's own fifty-two years. William married at an unusually early age. He was only eighteen, though his wife was twenty-six, almost exactly the norm of the day for women, though men normally married also in their mid- to late twenties. Shakespeare's wife Anne was already pregnant at the time that the marriage was formally confirmed, and a daughter, Susanna, was born six months later, in May 1583. Two years later, she gave birth to twins, Hamnet and Judith. Hamnet would die in his eleventh year.

If life was always at risk from what Shakespeare would later call "the thousand natural shocks / That flesh is heir to" (*Hamlet*, 3.1.61–62), the incessant threats to peace were no less unnerving, if usually less immediately life threatening. There were almost daily rumors of foreign invasion and civil war as the Protestant Queen Elizabeth assumed the crown in 1558 upon the death of her Catholic half sister, Mary. Mary's reign had been marked by the public burnings of Protestant "heretics," by the seeming subordination of England to Spain, and by a commitment to a ruinous war with France, that, among its other effects, fueled inflation and encouraged a debasing of the currency. If, for many, Elizabeth represented the hopes for a peaceful and prosperous Protestant future, it seemed unlikely in the early days of her rule that the young monarch could hold her England together against the twin menace of the powerful Catholic monarchies of Europe and the significant part of her own population who were reluctant to give up their old faith. No wonder the Queen's principal secretary saw England in the early years of Elizabeth's rule as a land surrounded by "perils many, great and imminent."

In Stratford-upon-Avon, it might often have been easy to forget what threatened from without. The simple rural life, shared by about 90 percent of the English populace, had its reassuring natural rhythms and delights. Life was structured by the daily rising and setting of the sun, and by the change of seasons. Crops were planted and harvested; livestock was bred, its young delivered; sheep were sheared, some livestock slaughtered. Market days and fairs saw the produce and crafts of the town arrayed as people came to sell and shop—and be entertained by musicians, dancers, and troupes of actors. But even in Stratford, the lurking tensions and dangers could be daily sensed. A few months before Shakespeare was born, there had been a shocking "defacing" of images in the church, as workmen, not content merely to whitewash over the religious paintings decorating the interior as they were ordered, gouged large holes in those felt to be too "Catholic"; a few months after Shakespeare's birth, the register of the same church records another deadly outbreak of plague. The sleepy market town on the northern bank of the gently flowing river Avon was not immune from the menace of the world that surrounded it.

This was the world into which Shakespeare was born. England at his birth was still poor and backward, a fringe nation on the periphery of Europe. English itself was a minor language, hardly spoken outside of the country's borders. Religious tension was inescapable, as the old Catholic faith was trying determinedly to hold on, even as Protestantism was once again anxiously trying to establish itself as the national religion. The country knew itself vulnerable to serious threats both from without and from within. In 1562, the young Queen, upon whom so many people's hopes rested, almost fell victim to smallpox, and in 1569 a revolt of the Northern earls tried to remove her from power and restore Catholicism as the national religion. The following year, Pope

Pius V pronounced the excommunication of "Elizabeth, the pretended queen of England" and forbade Catholic subjects obedience to the monarch on pain of their own excommunication. "Now we are in an evil way and going to the devil," wrote one clergyman, "and have all nations in our necks."

It was a world of dearth, danger, and domestic unrest. Yet it would soon dramatically change, and Shakespeare's literary contribution would, for future generations, come to be seen as a significant measure of England's remarkable transformation. In the course of Shakespeare's life, England, hitherto an unsophisticated and underdeveloped backwater acting as a bit player in the momentous political dramas taking place on the European continent, became a confident, prosperous, global presence. But this new world was only accidentally, as it is often known today, "The Age of Shakespeare." To the degree that historical change rests in the hands of any individual, credit must be given to the Queen. This new world arguably was "The Age of Elizabeth," even if it was not the Elizabethan Golden Age, as it has often been portrayed.

The young Queen quickly imposed her personality upon the nation. She had talented councilors around her, all with strong ties to her of friendship or blood, but the direction of government was her own. She was strong willed and cautious, certain of her right to rule and convinced that stability was her greatest responsibility. The result may very well have been, as historians have often charged, that important issues facing England were never dealt with head-on and left to her successors to settle, but it meant also that she was able to keep her England unified and for the most part at peace.

Religion posed her greatest challenge, though it is important to keep in mind that in this period, as an official at Elizabeth's court said, "Religion and the commonwealth cannot be parted asunder." Faith then was not the largely voluntary commitment it is today, nor was there any idea of some separation of church and state. Religion was literally a matter of life and death, of salvation and damnation, and the Church was the Church of England. Obedience to it was not only a matter of conscience but also of law. It was the single issue on which the nation was most likely to be torn apart.

Elizabeth's great achievement was that she was successful in ensuring that the Church of England became formally a Protestant Church, but she did so without either driving most of her Catholic subjects to sedition or alienating the more radical Protestant community. The so-called "Elizabethan Settlement" forged a broad Christian community of what has been called prayer-book Protestantism, even as many of its practitioners retained, as a clergyman said, "still a smack and savor of popish principles." If there were forces on both sides who were uncomfortable with the Settlement—committed Protestants, who wanted to do away with all vestiges of the old faith, and convinced Catholics, who continued to swear their allegiance to Rome—the majority of the country, as she hoped, found ways to live comfortably both within the law and within their faith. In 1571, she wrote to the Duke of Anjou that the forms of worship she recommended would "not properly compel any man to alter his opinion in the great matters now in controversy in the Church." The official toleration of religious ambiguity, as well as the familiar experience of an official change of state religion accompanying the crowning of a new monarch, produced a world where the familiar labels of Protestant and Catholic failed to define the forms of faith that most English people practiced. But for Elizabeth, most matters of faith could be left to individuals, as long as the Church itself, and Elizabeth's position at its head, would remain unchallenged.

In international affairs, she was no less successful with her pragmatism and willingness to pursue limited goals. A complex mix of prudential concerns about religion, the economy, and national security drove her foreign policy. She did not have imperial ambitions; in the main, she wanted only to be sure there would be no invasion of England and to encourage English trade. In the event, both goals brought England into conflict with Spain, determining the increasingly anti-Catholic tendencies of English foreign policy and, almost accidentally, England's emergence as a world power. When Elizabeth came to the throne, England was in many ways a mere satellite nation to the Netherlands, which was part of the Hapsburg Empire that the Catholic Philip II (who had briefly and unhappily been married to her predecessor and half sister, Queen Mary) ruled from Spain; by the end of her reign England was Spain's most bitter rival.

The transformation of Spain from ally to enemy came in a series of small steps (or missteps), no one of which was intended to produce what in the end came to pass. A series of posturings and provocations on both sides led to the rupture. In 1568, things moved to their breaking point, as the English confiscated a large shipment of gold that the Spanish were sending to their troops in the Netherlands. The following year saw the revolt of the Catholic earls in Northern England, followed by the papal excommunication of the Queen in 1570, both of which were by many in England assumed to be at the initiative, or at very least with the tacit support, of Philip. In fact he was not involved, but England under Elizabeth would never again think of Spain as a loyal friend or reliable ally. Indeed, Spain quickly became its mortal enemy. Protestant Dutch rebels had been opposing the Spanish domination of the Netherlands since the early 1560s, but, other than periodic financial support, Elizabeth had done little to encourage them. But in 1585, she sent troops under the command of the Earl of Leicester to support the Dutch rebels against the Spanish. Philip decided then to launch a full-scale attack on England, with the aim of deposing Elizabeth and restoring the Catholic faith. An English assault on Cadiz in 1587 destroyed a number of Spanish ships, postponing Philip's plans, but in the summer of 1588 the mightiest navy in the world, Philip's grand armada, with 132 ships and 30,493 sailors and troops, sailed for England.

By all rights, it should have been a successful invasion, but a combination of questionable Spanish tactics and a fortunate shift of wind resulted in one of England's greatest victories. The English had twice failed to intercept the armada off the coast of Portugal, and the Spanish fleet made its way to England, almost catching the English ships resupplying in Plymouth. The English navy was on its heels, when conveniently the Spanish admiral decided to anchor in the English Channel off the French port of Calais to wait for additional troops coming from the Netherlands. The English attacked with fireships, sinking four Spanish galleons, and strong winds from the south prevented an effective counterattack from the Spanish. The Spanish fleet was pushed into the North Sea, where it regrouped and decided its safest course was to attempt the difficult voyage home around Scotland and Ireland, losing almost half its ships on the way. For many in England the improbable victory was a miracle, evidence of God's favor for Elizabeth and the Protestant nation. Though war with Spain would not end for another fifteen years, the victory over the armada turned England almost overnight into a major world power, buoyed by confidence that they were chosen by God and, more tangibly, by a navy that could compete for control of the seas.

From a backward and insignificant Hapsburg satellite, Elizabeth's England had become, almost by accident, the leader of Protestant Europe. But if the victory over the armada signaled England's new place in the world, it hardly marked the end of England's travails. The economy, which initially was fueled by the military buildup, in the early 1590s fell victim to inflation, heavy taxation to support the war with Spain, the inevitable wartime disruptions of trade, as well as crop failures and a general economic downturn in Europe. Ireland, over which England had been attempting to impose its rule since 1168, continued to be a source of trouble and great expense (in some years costing the crown nearly one fifth of its total revenues). Even when the most organized of the rebellions, begun in 1594 and led by Hugh O'Neill, Earl of Tyrone, formally ended in 1603, peace and stability had not been achieved.

But perhaps the greatest instability came from the uncertainty over the succession, an uncertainty that marked Elizabeth's reign from its beginning. Her near death from smallpox in 1562 reminded the nation that an unmarried queen could not insure the succession, and Elizabeth was under constant pressure to marry and produce an heir. She was always aware of and deeply resented the pressure, announcing as early as 1559: "this shall be for me sufficient that a marble stone shall declare that a queen, having reigned such a time, lived and died a virgin." If, however, it was for her "sufficient," it was not so for her advisors and for much of the nation, who hoped she would wed. Arguably Elizabeth was the wiser, knowing that her unmarried hand was a political advantage, allowing her to diffuse threats or create alliances with the seeming possibility of a match. But as with so much in her reign, the strategy bought temporary stability at the price of longer-term solutions.

By the mid 1590s, it was clear that she would die unmarried and without an heir, and various candidates were positioning themselves to succeed her. Enough anxiety was produced that all published debate about the succession was forbidden by law. There was no direct descendant of the English crown to claim rule, and all the claimants had to reach well back into their family history to find some legitimacy. The best genealogical claim belonged to King James VI of Scotland. His mother, Mary, Queen of Scots, was the granddaughter of James IV of Scotland and Margaret Tudor, sister to Elizabeth's father, Henry VIII. Though James had right on his side, he was, it must be remembered, a foreigner. Scotland shared the island with England but was a separate nation. Great Britain, the union of England and Scotland, would not exist formally until 1707, but with Elizabeth's death early in the morning of March 24, 1603, surprisingly uneventfully the thirty-seven-year-old James succeeded to the English throne. Two nations, one king: King James VI of Scotland, King James I of England.

Most of his English subjects initially greeted the announcement of their new monarch with delight, relieved that the crown had successfully been transferred without any major disruption and reassured that the new King was married with two living sons. However, quickly many became disenchanted with a foreign King who spoke English with a heavy accent, and dismayed even further by the influx of Scots in positions of power. Nonetheless, the new King's greatest political liability may well have been less a matter of nationality than of temperament: he had none of Elizabeth's skill and ease in publicly wooing her subjects. The Venetian ambassador wrote back to the doge that the new King was unwilling to "caress the people, nor make them that good cheer the late Queen did, whereby she won their loves."

He was aloof and largely uninterested in the daily activities of governing, but he was interested in political theory and strongly committed to the cause of peace. Although a steadfast Protestant, he lacked the reflexive anti-Catholicism of many of his subjects. In England, he achieved a broadly consensual community of Protestants. The so-called King James Bible, the famous translation published first in 1611, was the result of a widespread desire to have an English Bible that spoke to all the nation, transcending the religious divisions that had placed three different translations in the hands of his subjects. Internationally, he styled himself *Rex Pacificus* (the peace-loving king). In 1604, the Treaty of London brought Elizabeth's war with Spain formally to an end, and over the next decade he worked to bring about political marriages that might cement stable alliances. In 1613, he married his daughter to the leader of the German Protestants, while the following year he began discussions with Catholic Spain to marry his son to the Infanta Maria. After some ten years of negotiations, James's hopes for what was known as the Spanish match were finally abandoned, much to the delight of the nation, whose long-felt fear and hatred for Spain outweighed the subtle political logic behind the plan.

But if James sought stability and peace, and for the most part succeeded in his aims (at least until 1618, when the bitter religio-political conflicts on the European continent swirled well out of the King's control), he never really achieved concord and cohesion. He ruled over two kingdoms that did not know, like, or even want to understand one another, and his rule did little to bring them closer together. His England remained separate from his Scotland, even as he ruled over both. And even his England remained self divided, as in truth it always was under Elizabeth, ever more a nation of prosperity and influence but still one forged out of deep-rooted divisions of means, faiths, and allegiances that made the very nature of English identity a matter of confusion and concern. Arguably this is the very condition of great drama—sufficient peace and prosperity to support a theater industry and sufficient provocation in the troubling uncertainties about what the nation was and what fundamentally mattered to its people to inspire plays that would offer tentative solutions or at the very least make the troubling questions articulate and moving.

Nine years before James would die in 1625, Shakespeare died, having returned from London to the small market town in which he was born. If London, now a thriving modern metropolis of well over 200,000 people, had, like the nation itself, been transformed in the course of his life, the Warwickshire market town still was much the same. The house in which Shakespeare was born still stood, as did the church in which he was baptized and the school in which he learned to read and write. The river Avon still ran slowly along the town's southern limits. What had changed was that Shakespeare was now its most famous citizen, and, although it would take more than another 100 years to fully achieve this, he would in time become England's, for having turned the great ethical, social, and political issues of his own age into plays that would live forever.

William Shakespeare: A Chronology

1558 **November 17: Queen Elizabeth crowned**

1564 April 26: Shakespeare baptized, third child born to John Shakespeare and Mary Arden

1564 **May 27: Death of Jean Calvin in Geneva**

1565 John Shakespeare elected alderman in Stratford-upon-Avon

1568 **Publication of the Bishops' Bible**

1568 September 4: John Shakespeare elected Bailiff of Stratford-upon-Avon

1569 **Northern Rebellion**

1570 **Queen Elizabeth excommunicated by the Pope**

1572 **August 24: St. Bartholomew's Day Massacre in Paris**

1576 **The Theatre is built in Shoreditch**

1577–1580 **Sir Francis Drake sails around the world**

1582 November 27: Shakespeare and Anne Hathaway married (Shakespeare is 18)

1583 Queen's Men formed

1583 May 26: Shakespeare's daughter, Susanna, baptized

1584 **Failure of the Virginia Colony**

1585 February 2: Twins, Hamnet and Judith, baptized (Shakespeare is 20)

1586 Babington Plot to dethrone Elizabeth and replace her with Mary, Queen of Scots

1587 February 8: Execution of Mary, Queen of Scots

1587 Rose Theatre built

1588 August: Defeat of the Spanish armada (Shakespeare is 24)

1588 September 4: Death of Robert Dudley, Earl of Leicester

1590 First three books of Spenser's *Faerie Queene* published; Marlowe's *Tamburlaine* published

1592 March 3: *Henry VI, Part One* performed at the Rose Theatre (Shakespeare is 27)

1593 February–November: Theaters closed because of plague

1593 Publication of *Venus and Adonis*

1594 Publication of *Titus Andronicus*, first play by Shakespeare to appear in print (though anonymously)

1594 Lord Chamberlain's Men formed

1595 March 15: Payment made to Shakespeare, Will Kemp, and Richard Burbage for performances at court in December, 1594

1595 Swan Theatre built

1596 Books 4–6 of *The Faerie Queene* published

1596 August 11: Burial of Shakespeare's son, Hamnet (Shakespeare is 32)

1596–1599 Shakespeare living in St. Helen's, Bishopsgate, London

1596 October 20: Grant of Arms to John Shakespeare

1597 May 4: Shakespeare purchases New Place, one of the two largest houses in Stratford (Shakespeare is 33)

1598 Publication of *Love's Labor's Lost*, first extant play with Shakespeare's name on the title page

1598 Publication of Francis Meres's *Palladis Tamia*, citing Shakespeare as "the best for Comedy and Tragedy" among English writers

1599 Opening of the Globe Theatre

1601 February 7: Lord Chamberlain's Men paid 40 shillings to play *Richard II* by supporters of the Earl of Essex, the day before his abortive rebellion

1601 February 17: Execution of Robert Devereaux, Earl of Essex

1601 September 8: Burial of John Shakespeare

1602 May 1: Shakespeare buys 107 acres of farmland in Stratford

1603 March 24: Queen Elizabeth dies; James VI of Scotland succeeds as James I of England (Shakespeare is 39)

1603 May 19: Lord Chamberlain's Men reformed as the King's Men

1604 Shakespeare living with the Mountjoys, a French Huguenot family, in Cripplegate, London

1604 First edition of Marlowe's *Dr. Faustus* published (written c. 1589)

1604 March 15: Shakespeare named among "players" given scarlet cloth to wear at royal procession of King James

1604 Publication of authorized version of *Hamlet* (Shakespeare is 40)

1605 Gunpowder Plot

1605 June 5: Marriage of Susanna Shakespeare to John Hall

1608 Publication of *King Lear* (Shakespeare is 44)

1608–1609 Acquisition of indoor Blackfriars Theatre by King's Men

1609 *Sonnets* published

1611 King James Bible published (Shakespeare is 47)

1612 November 6: Death of Henry, eldest son of King James

1613 February 14: Marriage of King James's daughter Elizabeth to Frederick, the Elector Palatine

1613 March 10: Shakespeare, with some associates, buys gatehouse in Blackfriars, London

1613 June 29: Fire burns the Globe Theatre

1614 Rebuilt Globe reopens

1616 February 10: Marriage of Judith Shakespeare to Thomas Quiney

1616 March 25: Shakespeare's will signed

1616 April 23: Shakespeare dies (age 52)

1616 April 23: Cervantes dies in Madrid

1616 April 25: Shakespeare buried in Holy Trinity Church in Stratford-upon-Avon

1623 August 6: Death of Anne Shakespeare

1623 October: Prince Charles, King James's son, returns from Madrid, having failed to arrange his marriage to Maria Anna, Infanta of Spain

1623 First Folio published with 36 plays (18 never previously published)

Words, Words, Words: Understanding Shakespeare's Language

by David Scott Kastan

It is silly to pretend that it is easy to read Shakespeare. Reading Shakespeare isn't like picking up a copy of *USA Today* or *The New Yorker*, or even F. Scott Fitzgerald's *Great Gatsby* or Toni Morrison's *Beloved*. It is hard work, because the language is often unfamiliar to us and because it is more concentrated than we are used to. In the theater it is usually a bit easier. Actors can clarify meanings with gestures and actions, allowing us to get the general sense of what is going on, if not every nuance of the language that is spoken. "Action is eloquence," as Volumnia puts it in *Coriolanus*, "and the eyes of th' ignorant / More learnèd than the ears" (3.276–277). Yet the real greatness of Shakespeare rests not on "the general sense" of his plays but on the specificity and suggestiveness of the words in which they are written. It is through language that the plays' full dramatic power is realized, and it is that rich and robust language, often pushed by Shakespeare to the very limits of intelligibility, that we must learn to understand. But we can come to understand it (and enjoy it), and this essay is designed to help.

Even experienced readers and playgoers need help. They often find that his words are difficult to comprehend. Shakespeare sometimes uses words no longer current in English or with meanings that have changed. He regularly multiplies words where seemingly one might do as well or even better. He characteristically writes sentences that are syntactically complicated and imaginatively dense. And it isn't just we, removed by some 400 years from his world, who find him difficult to read; in his own time, his friends and fellow actors knew Shakespeare was hard. As two of them, John Hemings and Henry Condell, put it in their prefatory remarks to Shakespeare's First Folio in 1623, "read him, therefore, and again and again; and if then you do not like him, surely you are in some manifest danger not to understand him."

From the very beginning, then, it was obvious that the plays both deserve and demand not only careful reading but continued re-reading—and that not to read Shakespeare with all the attention a reader can bring to bear on the language is almost to guarantee that a reader will not "understand him" and remain among those who "do not like him." But Shakespeare's colleagues were nonetheless confident that the plays exerted an attraction strong enough to ensure and reward the concentration of their readers, confident, as they say, that in them "you will find enough, both to draw and hold you." The plays do exert a kind of magnetic pull, and have successfully drawn in and held readers for over 400 years.

Once we are drawn in, we confront a world of words that does not always immediately yield its delights; but it will—once we learn to see what is demanded of us. Words in Shakespeare do a lot, arguably more than anyone else has ever asked them to do. In part, it is because he needed his words to do many things at once. His stage had no sets and few props, so his words are all we have to enable us to imagine what his characters see. And they also allow us to see what the characters don't see, especially about themselves. The words are vivid and immediate, as well as complexly layered and psychologically suggestive. The difficulties they pose are not the "thee's" and "thou's" or "prithee's" and "doth's" that obviously mark the chronological distance between Shakespeare and us. When Gertrude says to Hamlet, "thou hast thy father much offended"

(3.4.8), we have no difficulty understanding her chiding, though we might miss that her use of the "thou" form of the pronoun expresses an intimacy that Hamlet pointedly refuses with his reply: "Mother, *you* have my father much offended" (3.4.9; italics mine).

Most deceptive are words that look the same as words we know but now mean something different. Words often change meanings over time. When Horatio and the soldiers try to stop Hamlet as he chases after the Ghost, Hamlet pushes past them and says, "I'll make a ghost of him that lets me" (1.4.85). It seems an odd thing to say. Why should he threaten someone who "lets" him do what he wants to do? But here "let" means "hinder," not, as it does today, "allow" (although the older meaning of the word still survives, for example, in tennis, where a "let serve" is one that is hindered by the net on its way across). There are many words that can, like this, mislead us: "his" sometimes means "its," "an" often means "if," "envy" means something more like "malice," "cousin" means more generally "kinsman," and there are others, though all are easily defined. The difficulty is that we may not stop to look thinking we already know what the word means, but in this edition a ° following the word alerts a reader that there is a gloss in the left margin, and quickly readers get used to these older meanings.

Then, of course, there is the intimidation factor—strange, polysyllabic, or Latinate words that not only are foreign to us but also must have sounded strange even to Shakespeare's audiences. When Macbeth wonders whether all the water in all the oceans of the world will be able to clean his bloody hands after the murder of Duncan, he concludes: "No; this my hand will rather / The multitudinous seas incarnadine, / Making the green one red" (2.2.64–66). Duncan's blood staining Macbeth's murderous hand is so offensive that, not merely does it resist being washed off in water, but it will "the multitudinous seas incarnadine": that is, turn the sea-green oceans blood-red. Notes will easily clarify the meaning of the two odd words, but it is worth observing that they would have been as odd to Shakespeare's readers as they are to us. The *Oxford English Dictionary* (*OED*) shows no use of "multitudinous" before this, and it records no use of "incarnadine" before 1591 (*Macbeth* was written about 1606). Both are new words, coined from the Latin, part of a process in Shakespeare's time where English adopted many Latinate words as a mark of its own emergence as an important vernacular language. Here they are used to express the magnitude of Macbeth's offense, a crime not only against the civil law but also against the cosmic order, and then the simple monosyllables of turning "the green one red" provide an immediate (and needed) paraphrase and register his own sickening awareness of the true hideousness of his deed.

As with "multitudinous" in *Macbeth*, Shakespeare is the source of a great many words in English. Sometimes he coined them himself, or, if he didn't invent them, he was the first person whose writing of them has survived. Some of these words have become part of our language, so common that it is hard to imagine they were not always part of it: for example, "assassination" (*Macbeth*, 1.7.2), "bedroom" (*A Midsummer Night's Dream*, 2.2.57), "countless" (*Titus Andronicus*, 5.3.59), "fashionable" (*Troilus and Cressida*, 3.3.165), "frugal" (*The Merry Wives of Windsor*, 2.1.28), "laughable" (*The Merchant of Venice*, 1.1.56), "lonely" (*Coriolanus*, 4.1.30), and "useful" (*King John*, 5.2.81). But other words that he originated were not as, to use yet another Shakespearean coinage, "successful" (*Titus Andronicus*, 1.1.66). Words like "crimeless" (*Henry VI, Part Two*, 2.4.63, meaning "innocent"), "facinorous" (*All's Well That Ends Well*, 2.3.30, meaning "extremely wicked"), and "recountment" (*As You Like It*, 4.3.141, meaning "narrative" or "account") have, without much resistance, slipped into oblivion. Clearly Shakespeare liked words, even unwieldy ones. His working vocabulary, about 18,000 words, is staggering, larger than almost any other English writer, and he seems to be the first person to use in print about 1,000 of these. Whether he coined the new words himself or was intrigued by the new words he heard in the streets of London doesn't really matter; the point is that he was remarkably alert to and engaged with a dynamic language that was expanding in response to England's own expanding contact with the world around it.

But it is neither new words nor old ones that are the source of the greatest difficulty of Shakespeare's language. The real difficulty (and the real delight) comes in trying to see how he uses the words, how he endows them with more than their denotative meanings. Why, for example, does Macbeth say that he hopes that the "sure and firm-set earth" (2.1.56) will not hear his steps as he goes forward to murder Duncan? Here "sure" and "firm-set" mean virtually the same thing: stable, secure, fixed. Why use two words? If this were a student paper, no doubt the teacher would circle one of them and write "redundant." But the redundancy is exactly what Shakespeare wants. One word would do if the purpose were to describe the solidity of the earth, but here the redundancy points to something different. It reveals something about Macbeth's mind, betraying through the doubling how deep is his awareness of the world of stable values that the terrible act he is about to commit must unsettle.

Shakespeare's words usually work this way: in part describing what the characters see and as often betraying what they feel. The example from *Macbeth* is a simple example of how this works. Shakespeare's words are carefully patterned. How one says something is every bit as important as what is said, and the conspicuous patterns that are created alert us to the fact that something more than the words' lexical sense has been put into play. Words can be coupled, as in the example above, or knit into even denser metaphorical constellations to reveal something about the speaker (which often the speaker does not know), as in Prince Hal's promise to his father that he will outdo the rebels' hero, Henry Percy (Hotspur):

Percy is but my factor, good my lord,
To engross up glorious deeds on my behalf.
And I will call him to so strict account
That he shall render every glory up,
Yea, even the slightest worship of his time,
Or I will tear the reckoning from his heart.

(Henry IV, Part One, 3.2.147–152)

The Prince expresses his confidence that he will defeat Hotspur, but revealingly in a reiterated language of commercial exchange ("factor," "engross," "account," "render," "reckoning") that tells us something important both about the Prince and the ways in which he understands his world. In a play filled with references to coins and counterfeiting, the speech demonstrates not only that Hal has committed himself to the business at hand, repudiating his earlier, irresponsible tavern self, but also that he knows it is a business rather than a glorious world of chivalric achievement; he inhabits a world in which value (political as well as economic) is not intrinsic but determined by what people are willing to invest, and he proves himself a master of producing desire for what he has to offer.

Or sometimes it is not the network of imagery but the very syntax that speaks, as when Claudius announces his marriage to Hamlet's mother:

Therefore our sometime sister, now our Queen,
Th' imperial jointress to this warlike state,
Have we—as 'twere with a defeated joy,
With an auspicious and a dropping eye,
With mirth in funeral and with dole in marriage,
In equal scale weighing delight and dole—
Taken to wife. *(Hamlet, 1.2.8–14)*

All he really wants to say here is that he has married Gertrude, his former sister-in-law: "Therefore our sometime sister . . . Have we . . . Taken to wife." But the straightforward sentence gets interrupted and complicated, revealing his own discomfort with the announcement. His elaborations and intensifications of Gertrude's role ("sometime sister," "Queen," "imperial jointress"), the self-conscious rhetorical balancing of the middle three lines (indeed "in equal scale weighing delight and dole"), all declare by the all-too obvious artifice how desperate he is to hide the awkward facts behind a veneer of normalcy and propriety. The very unnaturalness of the sentence is what alerts us that we are meant to understand more than the simple relation of fact.

Why doesn't Shakespeare just say what he means? Well, he does—exactly what he means. In the example from *Hamlet* just above, Shakespeare shows us something about Claudius that Claudius doesn't know himself. Always Shakespeare's words will offer us an immediate sense of what is happening, allowing us to follow the action, but they also offer us a counterplot, pointing us to what might be behind the action, confirming or contradicting what the characters say. It is a language that shimmers with promise and possibility, opening the characters' hearts and minds to our view—and all we have to do is learn to pay attention to what is there before us.

Shakespeare's Verse

Another distinctive feature of Shakespeare's dramatic language is that much of it is in verse. Almost all of the plays mix poetry and prose, but the poetry dominates. *The Merry Wives of Windsor* has the lowest percentage (only about 13 percent verse), while *Richard II* and *King John* are written entirely in verse (the only examples, although *Henry VI, Part One* and *Part Three* have only a very few prose lines). In most of the plays, about 70 percent of the lines are written in verse.

Shakespeare's characteristic verse line is a non-rhyming iambic pentameter ("blank verse"), ten syllables with every second one stressed. In *A Midsummer Night's Dream*, Titania comes to her senses after a magic potion has led her to fall in love with an ass-headed Bottom: "Methought I was enamored of an ass" (4.1.76). Similarly, in *Romeo and Juliet*, Romeo gazes up at Juliet's window: "But soft, what light through yonder window breaks" (2.2.2). In both these examples, the line has ten syllables organized into five regular beats (each beat consisting of the stress on the second syllable of a pair, as in "But soft," the da-dum rhythm forming an "iamb"). Still, we don't hear these lines as jingles; they seem natural enough, in large part because this dominant pattern is varied in the surrounding lines.

The play of stresses indeed becomes another key to meaning, as Shakespeare alerts us to what is important. In *Measure for Measure*, Lucio urges Isabella to plead for her brother's life: "Oh, to him, to him, wench! He will relent" (2.2.129). The iambic norm (unstressed-stressed) tells us (and an actor) that the emphasis at the beginning of the line is on "to" not "him"—it is the action not the object that is being emphasized—and at the end of the line the stress falls on "will." Alternatively, the line can play against the established norm. In *Hamlet*, Claudius corrects Polonius's idea of what is bothering the Prince: "Love? His affections do not that way tend" (3.1.161). The iambic norm forces the emphasis onto "that" ("do not *that* way tend"), while the syntax forces an unexpected stress on the opening word, "Love." In the famous line, "The course of true love never did run smooth" (*A Midsummer Night's Dream*, 1.1.134), the iambic expectation is varied in both the middle and at the end of the line. Both "love" and the first syllable of "never" are stressed, as are both syllables at the end: "run smooth," creating a metrical foot in which both syllables are stressed (called a "spondee"). The point to notice is that the "da-dum, da-dum, da-dum, da-dum, da-dum" line is not inevitable; it merely sets an expectation against which many variations can be heard.

In fact, even the ten-syllable norm can be varied. Shakespeare sometimes writes lines with fewer or more syllables. Often there is an extra, unstressed syllable at the end of a line (a so-called "feminine ending"); sometimes there are verse lines with only nine. In *Henry IV, Part One*, King Henry replies incredulously to the rebel Worcester's claim that he hadn't "sought" the confrontation with the King: "You have not sought it. How comes it then?" (5.1.27). There are only nine syllables here (some earlier editors, seeking to "correct" the verse, added the word "sir" after the first question to regularize the line). But the pause where one expects a stressed syllable is dramatically effective, allowing the King's anger to be powerfully present in the silence.

As even these few examples show, Shakespeare's verse is unusually flexible, allowing a range of rhythmical effects. It should not be understood as a set of strict rules but as a flexible set of practices rooted in dramatic necessity. It is designed to highlight ideas and emotions, and it is based less upon rigid syllable counts than on an arrangement of stresses within an understood temporal norm, as one might expect from a poetry written to be heard in the theater rather than read on the page.

Here Follows Prose

Although the plays are dominated by verse, prose plays a significant role. Shakespeare's prose has its own rhythms, but it lacks the formal patterning of verse, and so is printed without line breaks and without the capitals that mark the beginning of a verse line. Like many of his fellow dramatists, Shakespeare tended to use prose for comic scenes, the shift from verse serving, especially in his early plays, as a social marker. Upper-class characters speak in verse; lower-class characters speak in prose. Thus, in *A Midsummer Night's Dream*, the Athenians of the court, as well as the fairies, all speak in verse, but the "rude mechanicals," Bottom and his artisan friends, all speak in prose, except for the comic verse they speak in their performance of "Pyramis and Thisbe."

As Shakespeare grew in experience, he became more flexible about the shifts from verse to prose, letting it, among other things, mark genre rather than class and measure various kinds of intensity. Prose becomes in the main the medium of comedy. The great comedies, like *Much Ado About Nothing*, *Twelfth Night*, and *As You Like It*, are all more than 50 percent prose. But even in comedy, shifts between verse and prose may be used to measure subtle emotional changes. In Act One, scene three of *The Merchant of Venice*, Shylock and Bassanio begin the scene speaking of matters of business in prose, but when Antonio enters and the deep conflict between the Christian and the Jew becomes evident, the scene shifts to verse. But prose may itself serve in moments of emotional intensity. Shylock's famous speech in Act Three, scene one, "Hath not a Jew eyes . . ." is all in prose, as is Hamlet's expression of disgust at the world ("I have of late—but wherefore I know not—lost all my mirth . . .") at 3.1.261–276. Shakespeare comes to use prose to vary the tone of a scene, as the shift from verse subtly alerts an audience or a reader to some new emotional register.

Prose becomes, as Shakespeare's art matures, not inevitably the mark of the lower classes but the mark of a salutary daily-ness. It is appropriately the medium in which letters are written, and it is the medium of a common sense that will at least challenge the potential self-deceptions of grandiloquent speech. When Rosalind mocks the excesses and artifice of Orlando's wooing in Act Four, scene one of *As You Like It*, it is in prose that she seeks something genuine in the expression of love:

> The poor world is almost six thousand years old, and in all this time there was not any man died in his own person, *videlicit* [i.e., namely], in a love cause. . . . Men have died from time to time, and worms have eaten them, but not for love.

Here the prose becomes the sound of common sense, an effective foil to the affectation of pinning poems to trees and thinking that it is real love.

It is not that prose is artless; Shakespeare's prose is no less self-conscious than his verse. The artfulness of his prose is different, of course. The seeming ordinariness of his prose is no less an effect of his artistry than is the more obvious patterning of his verse. Prose is no less serious, compressed, or indeed figurative. As with his verse, Shakespeare's prose performs numerous tasks and displays various, subtle formal qualities; and recognizing the possibilities of what it can achieve is still another way of seeing what Shakespeare puts right before us to show us what he has hidden.

Further Reading

N.F. Blake, *Shakespeare's Language: An Introduction* (New York: St. Martin's Press, 1983).

Jonathan Hope, *Shakespeare's Grammar* (London: Thomson, 2003).

Sister Miriam Joseph, *Shakespeare's Use of the Arts of Language* (New York: Columbia University Press, 1947).

M. M. Mahood, *Shakespeare's Wordplay* (London: Methuen, 1957).

Russ McDonald, *Shakespeare and the Arts of Language* (Oxford: Oxford University Press, 2001).

Brian Vickers, *The Artistry of Shakespeare's Prose* (London: Methuen, 1968).

George T. Wright, *Shakespeare's Metrical Art* (Berkeley: Univ. of California Press, 1991).

Key to the Play Text

Symbols

°	Indicates an explanation or definition in the left-hand margin.
1	Indicates a gloss on the page facing the play text.
[ ]	Indicates something added or changed by the editors (i.e., not in the early printed text that this edition of the play is based on).

Terms

Q, Quarto	An edition of the play printed in 1600, and the basis for this edition (see Editing *Much Ado About Nothing*, p. 305).
F, Folio, or *First Folio*	The first collected edition of Shakespeare's plays, published in 1623.

Much Ado About Nothing

William Shakespeare

List of Roles

Don Pedro	*Prince of Aragon*
Don John	*illegitimate brother of Don Pedro*
Signior Benedick	*a lord of Padua*
Signior Claudio	*a lord of Florence*
Balthasar	*Don Pedro's attendant*
Conrade **Borachio** }	*Don John's followers*
Leonato	*Governor of Messina*
Innogen	*wife of Leonato*
Antonio	*brother of Leonato*
Hero	*daughter of Leonato*
Beatrice	*orphaned niece of Leonato*
Margaret **Ursula** }	*Hero's waiting women*
Friar Francis	
Dogberry	*master constable*
Verges	*a headborough (a petty constable)*
George Seacole	*a member of the watch*
First Watchman	
Boy	*Benedick's servant*
Messengers	

Lords, kinsmen, attendants, watchmen, and musicians

1 **Innogen**, his wife

Most editors omit this character because she has no lines in this scene or in 2.1, where the stage direction calls for the entrance of *Leonato, his brother, his wife*, and because she is not named in the stage directions for the wedding scene (4.1). Yet, Innogen, mother of the normally taciturn Hero, could be an interesting silent presence and is named in both the Quarto and Folio texts.

2 *Aragon*

A region in northeast Spain

3 *Messina*

Shakespeare here announces the location as Italy, specifically Sicily, a stereotypical place of intrigues and jealous lovers. Created by travelers' tales and the fictions of the novella, Italy provided a perfect setting for tragedies of love—*Romeo and Juliet* and *Othello*—as well as for comedies and romances—*The Merchant of Venice, All's Well That Ends Well, Cymbeline*, and *The Winter's Tale*. For the thematic associations of Italy, see Michael J. Redmond in the For Further Reading section.

4 *three leagues*

I.e., about nine miles (a *league* is a unit of length measuring roughly three miles)

5 *equally remembered*

Appropriately rewarded

6 *doing in the figure of a lamb*

I.e., accomplishing while appearing (*in the figure of*) so young and inexperienced (like *a lamb*)

7 *uncle*

There is no further mention of this relative.

8 *even so much that joy could not show itself modest enough without a badge of bitterness*

So much joy that he needed some mark of sadness so his expression of delight would not seem inappropriate. *A badge of bitterness* refers to the badges, worn by servants, that expressed their household affiliation and their inferior social position.

Act 1, Scene 1

Enter **Leonato**, *Governor of Messina;* **Innogen**, *his wife;*[1] **Hero**, *his daughter; and* **Beatrice** *his niece, with a* **Messenger**.

Leonato

I learn in this letter that Don Pedro of Aragon[2] comes this night to Messina.[3]

Messenger

i.e., now He is very near by this.° He was not three leagues[4] off when I left him.

Leonato

battle How many gentlemen have you lost in this action?°

Messenger

distinction / nobility But few of any sort,° and none of name.°

Leonato

A victory is twice itself when the achiever brings home full numbers. I find here that Don Pedro hath bestowed much honor on a young Florentine called Claudio.

Messenger

i.e. Claudio's Much deserved on his° part, and equally remembered[5] by Don Pedro. He hath borne himself beyond the promise of his age, doing in the figure of a lamb[6] the *surpassed* feats of a lion. He hath indeed better bettered° expectation than you must expect of me to tell you how.

Leonato

He hath an uncle[7] here in Messina will be very much glad of it.

Messenger

I have already delivered him letters, and there appears much joy in him—even so much that joy could not *moderate* show itself modest° enough without a badge of bitterness.[8]

1 *kindness*

Familial affection

2 *Montanto*

Fencing term for an upward thrust, used here ironically by Beatrice

3 *Padua*

A city in northern Italy

4 *challenged Cupid at the flight*

Challenged Cupid to an archery match; a *flight* arrow is a light arrow for long-distance shooting.

5 *subscribed for Cupid*

Took up the challenge (literally signed up or *subscribed*) on Cupid's behalf

6 *bird-bolt*

Short, blunt arrow used by children (and therefore by Cupid, who is usually depicted as a child)

Leonato

Did he break out into tears?

Messenger

In great measure.

Leonato

natural A kind° overflow of kindness.[1] There are no faces truer than those that are so washed. How much better is it to weep at joy than to joy at weeping!

Beatrice

I pray you, is Signior Montanto[2] returned from the wars or no?

Messenger

I know none of that name, lady. There was none such in the army of any sort.

Leonato

What is he that you ask for, niece?

Hero

My cousin means Signior Benedick of Padua.[3]

Messenger

merry Oh, he's returned, and as pleasant° as ever he was.

Beatrice

posters He set up his bills° here in Messina and challenged
Jester Cupid at the flight,[4] and my uncle's fool,° reading the challenge, subscribed for Cupid[5] and challenged
i.e., Benedick him at the bird-bolt.[6] I pray you, how many hath he° killed and eaten in these wars? But how many hath he killed? For indeed I promised to eat all of his killing.

Leonato

criticize Faith, niece, you tax° Signior Benedick too much,
even but he'll be meet° with you, I doubt it not.

Messenger

He hath done good service, lady, in these wars.

1 *musty victual*

Moldy food

2 *stuffed man*

I.e., scarecrow; dummy stuffed with rags or straw to look like a man

3 *But for the stuffing—well, we are all mortal.*

But as for (what) the *stuffing* (is made of)—well, we all have our faults.

4 *nothing*

The first instance of this key word from the play's title. *Nothing* is, in addition to its obvious meaning, a homonym for "noting," i.e., observing (including eavesdropping), and assigning blame. *Nothing* is also Elizabethan slang for female genitals. The play's title is a proverbial expression (cf. *As You Like It*; *All's Well That Ends Well*; *Twelfth Night, or What You Will*).

5 *five wits*

The five mental faculties: fantasy, memory, imagination, judgment, and common sense

6 *wit enough to keep himself warm*

I.e., enough common sense

7 *bear it for a difference*

I.e., use it to mark the distinction; a *difference* is a technical heraldic term for an alteration in a coat of arms that distinguishes different branches of a noble family.

8 *for it is all the wealth that he hath left to be known a reasonable creature*

For it (his remaining wit) is all he has left to mark him as a rational being (rather than a beast)

9 *next block*

New form for shaping a hat; therefore, the latest fashion

Beatrice

helped *eater* *appetite*

You had musty victual,[1] and he hath holp° to eat it. He is a very valiant trencherman;° he hath an excellent stomach.°

Messenger

And a good soldier too, lady.

Beatrice

in comparison with

And a good soldier to° a lady, but what is he to a lord?

Messenger

A lord to a lord, a man to a man, stuffed with all honorable virtues.

Beatrice

It is so indeed. He is no less than a stuffed man.[2] But for the stuffing—well, we are all mortal.[3]

Leonato

except

You must not, sir, mistake my niece. There is a kind of merry war betwixt Signior Benedick and her. They never meet but° there's a skirmish of wit between them.

Beatrice

limping

Alas, he gets nothing[4] by that. In our last conflict four of his five wits[5] went halting° off, and now is the whole man governed with one; so that if he have wit enough to keep himself warm,[6] let him bear it for a difference[7] between himself and his horse, for it is all the wealth that he hath left to be known a reasonable creature.[8] Who is his companion now? He hath every month a new sworn brother.

Messenger

Is 't possible?

Beatrice

loyalty

Very easily possible. He wears his faith° but as the fashion of his hat; it ever changes with the next block.[9]

1 *I will hold friends with you, lady.*

I will stay friendly with you (in order to avoid your wit).

2 *run-mad*

Referring back to line 74, Leonato predicts that Beatrice will never succumb to Benedick's charms.

3 *is approached*

Has arrived

4 *cost*

Expense. Leonato takes on an enormous expense in hosting the army.

Messenger

favor I see, lady, the gentleman is not in your books.°

Beatrice

If/library No. An° he were, I would burn my study.° But I pray
you, who is his companion? Is there no young
hothead squarer° now that will make a voyage with him to the
devil?

Messenger

He is most in the company of the right noble Claudio.

Beatrice

i.e., Benedick O Lord, he° will hang upon him like a disease! He is
plague / infected person sooner caught than the pestilence,° and the taker°
immediately runs presently° mad. God help the noble Claudio! If he
have caught the Benedick, it will cost him a thousand
he pound ere 'a° be cured.

Messenger

I will hold friends with you, lady.[1]

Beatrice

Do, good friend.

Leonato

You will never run mad,[2] niece.

Beatrice

No, not till a hot January.

Messenger

Don Pedro is approached.[3]

Enter **Don Pedro**, **Claudio**, **Benedick**, **Balthasar**, *and* [**Don**] **John** *the bastard.*

Don Pedro

Good Signior Leonato, are you come to meet your
custom trouble? The fashion° of the world is to avoid cost,[4]
come to meet and you encounter° it.

1 *trouble being gone, comfort should remain, but when you depart from me, sorrow abides and happiness takes his leave*

Normally when *trouble* has departed, contentment is what remains, but when you leave, *happiness* departs, and sorrow stays behind.

2 *for then were you a child*

When Hero was born, you were *a child* (and therefore could not be Hero's father). Leonato jokes about Benedick's reputation as a womanizer, and the exchange (lines 89–93) is the first of the play's many references to possible infidelity.

3 *You have it full*

You are fully repaid (for your witticism).

4 *fathers herself*

Makes apparent who her father is (by her resemblance to him)

5 *are like*

Resemble

6 *would not have his head on her shoulders*

Would not want to resemble his aged features too exactly

Leonato

Never came trouble to my house in the likeness of your Grace; for trouble being gone, comfort should remain, but when you depart from me, sorrow abides and happiness takes his° leave.[1]

its

Don Pedro

You embrace your charge° too willingly. I think this is your daughter.

duty

Leonato

Her mother hath many times told me so.

Benedick

Were you in doubt, sir, that you asked her?

Leonato

Signior Benedick, no, for then were you a child.[2]

Don Pedro

You have it full,[3] Benedick. We may guess by this° what you are, being a man. Truly, the lady fathers herself.[4] —Be happy, lady, for you are like[5] an honorable father.

i.e., Leonato's comment

[**Leonato** *and* **Don Pedro** *continue talking privately.*]

Benedick

If Signior Leonato be her father, she would not have his head on her shoulders[6] for all Messina, as like him as she is.

Beatrice

I wonder that you will still° be talking, Signior Benedick; nobody marks° you.

always

pays attention to

Benedick

What, my dear Lady Disdain! Are you yet living?

Beatrice

Is it possible disdain should die while she hath such meet° food to feed it as Signior Benedick? Courtesy

suitable

1 *cold blood I am of your humor*

A reference to the theory that humans were composed of four humors or fluids (blood, phlegm, yellow bile, or black bile) and that the proportion of these elements, variously hot or cold, moist or dry, determined complexion and character. A predominance of blood (warm and moist) created a sanguine character, for example: courageous, cheerful, ruddy in countenance, and amorous in temperament. Beatrice describes her blood as *cold* and therefore unnaturally opposed to love. A predominance of black bile created a melancholy character. Hero says that Don John has a *melancholy disposition* (2.1.5); Benedick finds the depressed Claudio *melancholy* (2.1.188); the *pleasant-spirited* Beatrice has *little of the melancholy element in her* (2.1.306).

2 *parrot teacher*

I.e., blatherer; as repetitive as one training a *parrot* to speak

3 *A bird of my tongue is better than a beast of yours.*

A *bird* who has my way with words is better than a *beast* who cannot speak at all, like you.

4 *so good a continuer*

Had the same stamina running (as you do talking)

5 *jade's trick*

A trick used by a willful horse (*jade*) to unseat its rider, in this case stopping suddenly

6 *of old*

From before; well

turn itself must convert° to disdain if you come in her presence.

Benedick

Then is courtesy a turncoat. But it is certain I am loved of° all ladies, only you excepted. And I would° I could find in my heart that I had not a hard heart, for truly I love none. *by / wish*

Beatrice

A dear happiness to women. They would else have been troubled with a pernicious suitor. I thank God and my cold blood I am of your humor[1] for that. I had rather hear my dog bark at a crow than a man swear he loves me.

Benedick

always God keep your Ladyship still° in that mind, so some *unavoidable; fated* gentleman or other shall 'scape a predestinate° scratched face.

Beatrice

if Scratching could not make it worse an° 'twere such a face as yours were.

Benedick

extraordinary Well, you are a rare° parrot teacher.[2]

Beatrice

A bird of my tongue is better than a beast of yours.[3]

Benedick

I would my horse had the speed of your tongue and so good a continuer.[4] But keep your way, i' God's name. I have done.

Beatrice

You always end with a jade's trick.[5] I know you of old.[6]

[**Leonato** *and* **Don Pedro** *move forward.*]

1 *you shall not be forsworn*

I.e., I won't do anything to make you a liar.

2 *Your hand, Leonato. We will go together.*

By taking Leonato's hand, Don Pedro declines Leonato's offer to let him enter first.

3 *noted her not*

Did not take special notice of her (but see page 50, note 4).

Don Pedro

That is the sum of all, Leonato.—Signior Claudio and Signior Benedick, my dear friend Leonato hath invited you all. I tell him we shall stay here at the least a month, and he heartily prays some occasion may detain us longer. I dare swear he is no hypocrite but prays from his heart.

Leonato

If you swear, my lord, you shall not be forsworn.[1]

Since you are [*to* **Don John**] Let me bid you welcome, my lord. Being° reconciled to the Prince your brother, I owe you all duty.

Don John

I thank you. I am not of many words, but I thank you.

Leonato

Please it your Grace lead on?

Don Pedro

Your hand, Leonato. We will go together.[2]

They exit, [except for] **Benedick** *and* **Claudio**.

Claudio

Benedick, didst thou note the daughter of Signior Leonato?

Benedick

I noted her not,[3] but I looked on her.

Claudio

Is she not a modest young lady?

Benedick

Do you question me as an honest man should do, for my simple true judgment? Or would you have me

i.e., enemy speak after my custom, as being a professed tyrant° to their sex?

1 *do you play the flouting jack, to tell us Cupid is a good hare-finder and Vulcan a rare carpenter*

I.e., are you being a sarcastic knave (*flouting jack*) by offering praise obviously contrary to fact? Blind *Cupid* would be poor at spotting hares, and *Vulcan* is the Roman god of blacksmiths.

2 *possessed with a fury*

In a passionate rage; literally, controlled by one of the goddesses (Erinyes or Furies), who avenged crimes by driving the wrongdoers mad

Claudio

No. I pray thee speak in sober judgment.

Benedick

short Why, i' faith, methinks she's too low° for a high praise, too brown for a fair praise, and too little for a great praise. Only this commendation I can afford her: that were she other than she is, she were unhandsome, and, being no other but as she is, I do not like her.

Claudio

jest Thou thinkest I am in sport.° I pray thee tell me truly how thou lik'st her.

Benedick

Would you buy her, that you enquire after her?

Claudio

Can the world buy such a jewel?

Benedick

Yea, and a case to put it into. But speak you this with a *serious* sad° brow? Or do you play the flouting jack, to tell us Cupid is a good hare-finder and Vulcan a rare *understand* carpenter?[1] Come; in what key shall a man take° *join* you to go° in the song?

Claudio

In mine eye she is the sweetest lady that ever I looked on.

Benedick

I can see yet without spectacles, and I see no such *if* matter. There's her cousin, an° she were not possessed with a fury,[2] exceeds her as much in beauty as the first of May doth the last of December. But I hope you have no intent to turn husband, have you?

Claudio

I would scarce trust myself, though I had sworn the contrary, if Hero would be my wife.

1 *hath not the world one man but he will wear his cap with suspicion?*

I.e., isn't there one man alive who isn't ready to get married? Benedick, however, characteristically expresses this as a question about every man's willingness to be a cuckold (a betrayed husband), often imagined with horns and wearing a *cap* to hide them. Benedick continues the jokes about horns throughout this scene. In lines 210–211, for example, he asks women to pardon him for refusing to have *a recheat winded in my forehead* (a hunting call sounded on his horn), and to *hang my bugle in an invisible baldrick* (to keep his horn on its invisible strap on his head). As many have observed, male anxiety about cuckoldry runs throughout the play, motivating the plot against Hero. See Berger, McEachern, and Neely in the For Further Reading section.

2 *Go to*

An expression of impatience or disbelief, like the modern "get out of here" or "go on"

3 *wear the print of it and sigh away Sundays*

I.e., bear the burden and drudgery of married life so even your leisure time is dull

4 *so were it uttered*

That is how he would put it.

5 *Like the old tale, my lord: "It is not so nor 'twas not so but, indeed, God forbid it should be so."*

Benedick quotes a folktale in which a bridegroom repeatedly uses this line to defend himself to his fiancée, who uncovers incontrovertible evidence that he is a thief.

Benedick

sixty (years) / *if* / *imprint*

Is 't come to this? In faith, hath not the world one man but he will wear his cap with suspicion?[1] Shall I never see a bachelor of three-score° again? Go to,[2] i' faith. An° thou wilt needs thrust thy neck into a yoke, wear the print° of it and sigh away Sundays.[3] Look, Don Pedro is returned to seek you.

Enter **Don Pedro**.

Don Pedro

What secret hath held you here that you followed not to Leonato's?

Benedick

compel

I would your Grace would constrain° me to tell.

Don Pedro

I charge thee on thy allegiance.

Benedick

as secretive / mute

You hear, Count Claudio? I can be secret° as a dumb° man, I would have you think so, but on my allegiance—mark you this, on my allegiance—[*to* **Don Pedro**] he is in love. With who? Now, that is your Grace's part. Mark how short his answer is: with Hero, Leonato's short daughter.

Claudio

If this were so, so were it uttered.[4]

Benedick

Like the old tale, my lord: "It is not so nor 'twas not so but, indeed, God forbid it should be so."[5]

Claudio

If my passion change not shortly, God forbid it should be otherwise.

1 *fetch me in*

I.e., get me to confess

2 *my two faiths and troths*

I.e., by my allegiance to Don Pedro and Claudio, with an implicit joke about dual allegiances implying duplicity

3 *I will die in it at the stake.*

Even if I were burned *at the stake*, I would not renounce this conviction.

4 *heretic*

Heretics (those who refused to accept the central tenets of the Church) could be burned at the stake, hence Don Pedro's joking reference here to Benedick's refusal to acknowledge Beatrice's attractiveness.

5 *And never could maintain his part but in the force of his will.*

And could only hold his belief by sheer stubbornness

6 *that I will have a recheat winded in my forehead or hang my bugle in an invisible baldrick, all women shall pardon me*

A *recheat* is the notes played (*winded*) on a horn to announce the beginning or end of a hunt, while a *baldrick* is a belt; the line means, therefore, something like: I will not wear the horns of a cuckold or have my dignity depend on something that can't be verified (i.e., the fidelity of a woman).

Don Pedro

Amen, if you love her, for the lady is very well worthy.

Claudio

You speak this to fetch me in,[1] my lord.

Don Pedro

faith By my troth,° I speak my thought.

Claudio

And, in faith, my lord, I spoke mine.

Benedick

And by my two faiths and troths,[2] my lord, I spoke mine.

Claudio

That I love her, I feel.

Don Pedro

That she is worthy, I know.

Benedick

That I neither feel how she should be loved nor know how she should be worthy is the opinion that fire cannot melt out of me. I will die in it at the stake.[3]

Don Pedro

scorn Thou wast ever an obstinate heretic[4] in the despite° of beauty.

Claudio

And never could maintain his part but in the force of his will.[5]

Benedick

That a woman conceived me, I thank her. That she brought me up, I likewise give her most humble thanks. But that I will have a recheat winded in my forehead or hang my bugle in an invisible baldrick, all women shall pardon me.[6] Because I will not do them the wrong to mistrust any, I will do myself *conclusion* the right to trust none. And the fine° is, for the

1 *go the finer*

Dress better (because he will be without the expenses of a wife)

2 *lose more blood with love than I will get again with drinking*

It was thought that the sighs of love drew blood from the heart, and that drinking wine replenished it.

3 *ballad-maker's pen*

A pen used for writing love ballads

4 *the sign of blind Cupid*

A signboard painted with a picture of Cupid

5 *hang me in a bottle like a cat and shoot at me*

I.e., Use me for target practice. Archers were said to use cats in baskets (*bottles*) for target practice.

6 *Adam*

A reference to the renowned archer Adam Bell

7 *In time the savage bull doth bear the yoke.*

The phrase is proverbial but may have been borrowed directly from Thomas Kyd's *Spanish Tragedy* (c. 1587), "In time the savage bull sustains the yoke" (2.1.3); i.e., eventually even the most aggressive bull will end up pulling a plow.

8 *pluck off the bull's horns and set them in my forehead*

Another allusion to the cuckold's horns

9 *horn-mad*

(1) enraged; (2) mad with jealousy

10 *Venice*

Venice was renowned for its courtesans.

11 *quake*

Tremble (a conventional sign of lovesickness), punning on *quiver* in the previous line, which also could mean "tremble" in addition to a "case for arrows" as it does there

which I may go the finer,[1] I will live a bachelor.

Don Pedro

I shall see thee, ere I die, look pale with love.

Benedick

With anger, with sickness, or with hunger, my lord, not with love. Prove° that ever I lose more blood with love than I will get again with drinking,[2] pick out mine eyes with a ballad-maker's pen[3] and hang me up at the door of a brothel house for the sign of blind Cupid.[4]

If you prove

Don Pedro

Well, if ever thou dost fall from this faith, thou wilt prove a notable argument.°

subject of conversation

Benedick

If I do, hang me in a bottle like a cat and shoot at me,[5] and he that hits me, let him be clapped on the shoulder and called Adam.[6]

Don Pedro

Well, as time shall try.° In time the savage bull doth bear the yoke.[7]

reveal

Benedick

The savage bull may, but if ever the sensible Benedick bear it, pluck off the bull's horns and set them in my forehead,[8] and let me be vilely painted, and, in such great letters as they write "Here is good horse to hire," let them signify under my sign:° "Here you may see Benedick the married man."

image

Claudio

If this should ever happen, thou wouldst be horn-mad.[9]

Don Pedro

Nay, if Cupid have not spent all his quiver° in Venice,[10] thou wilt quake[11] for this shortly.

i.e., of arrows

1 *I look for an earthquake too*

I.e., an earthquake is as probable.

2 *temporize with the hours*

Compromise (i.e., grow more realistic) with the passing of time

3 *To the tuition of God. From my house if I had it—/The sixth of July. Your loving friend, Benedick.*

Claudio and Don Pedro mock Benedick's departure, which sounds like the formal closing of a letter.

4 *The body of your discourse is sometime guarded with fragments, and the guards are but slightly basted on neither.*

Benedick accuses Claudio and Don Pedro of being guilty of the same rhetorical excess that they have just charged him with indulging. Benedick employs a tailoring metaphor, comparing the material of Claudio's and Don Pedro's speeches to a dress that has been ridiculously adorned with superfluous, loosely stitched embellishments.

5 *old ends*

Clichés

Benedick

I look for an earthquake too,[1] then.

Don Pedro

Well, you will temporize with the hours.[2] In the mean-
go time, good Signior Benedick, repair° to Leonato's.
Commend me to him and tell him I will not fail him at
supper, for indeed he hath made great preparation.

Benedick

intelligence I have almost matter° enough in me for such an
mission embassage,° and so I commit you—

Claudio

protection To the tuition° of God. From my house, if I had it—

Don Pedro

The sixth of July. Your loving friend, Benedick.[3]

Benedick

Nay, mock not; mock not. The body of your discourse
adorned is sometime guarded° with fragments, and the guards
mock are but slightly basted on neither.[4] Ere you flout° old
ends[5] any further, examine your conscience. And so I
leave you. *He exits.*

Claudio

My liege, your Highness now may do me good.

Don Pedro

My love is thine to teach. Teach it but how,
And thou shalt see how apt it is to learn
Any hard lesson that may do thee good.

Claudio

Hath Leonato any son, my lord?

Don Pedro

No child but Hero; she's his only heir.
desire Dost thou affect° her, Claudio?

1 *ended action*

Recently completed military campaign

2 *a book of words*

I.e., such long speeches

3 *break with her*

Broach the subject to her

4 *his complexion*

Its appearance

5 *salved it with a longer treatise*

Smoothed over (its impropriety) by speaking at greater length

6 *The fairest grant is the necessity.*

The best gift is that which is needed.

7 *Look what*

Whatever

8 *in her bosom I'll unclasp my heart*

In private I will open my heart (as if I were you).

Claudio

O my lord,
When you went onward on this ended action,[1]
I looked upon her with a soldier's eye
That liked but had a rougher task in hand
convert Than to drive° liking to the name of love.
now that But now° I am returned, and that war thoughts
place Have left their places vacant, in their rooms°
Come thronging soft and delicate desires,
All prompting me how fair young Hero is,
Saying I liked her ere I went to wars.

Don Pedro

in no time Thou wilt be like a lover presently°
And tire the hearer with a book of words.[2]
If thou dost love fair Hero, cherish it,
And I will break with her[3] and with her father,
And thou shalt have her. Was 't not to this end
spin That thou began'st to twist° so fine a story?

Claudio

How sweetly you do minister to love,
That know love's grief by his complexion![4]
But lest my liking might too sudden seem,
I would have salved it with a longer treatise.[5]

Don Pedro

river What need the bridge much broader than the flood?°
The fairest grant is the necessity.[6]
once and for all Look what[7] will serve is fit. 'Tis once:° thou lovest,
provide And I will fit° thee with the remedy.
a masked ball I know we shall have reveling° tonight.
identity I will assume thy part° in some disguise
And tell fair Hero I am Claudio,
And in her bosom I'll unclasp my heart[8]

1 *I will assume thy part in some disguise / And tell fair Hero I am Claudio, / And in her bosom I'll unclasp my heart / And take her hearing prisoner with the force / And strong encounter of my amorous tale. / Then after to her father will I break, / And the conclusion is, she shall be thine.*

Don Pedro here promises to disguise himself as Claudio, woo Hero, then tell her father the truth and relinquish her to the real Claudio. In the next scene, Antonio delivers a garbled version of the plan to Leonato, based on the report of his eavesdropping servant: *the Prince discovered to Claudio that he loved my niece your daughter and meant to acknowledge it this night in a dance, and, if he found her accordant, he meant to take the present time by the top and instantly break with you of it* (1.2.10–14); the eavesdropping Borachio reports to Don John still another version of the plot: *the Prince should woo Hero for himself, and, having obtained her, give her to Count Claudio* (1.3.53–54). Despite this report, Don John tells Claudio (disguised as Benedick) a lie that largely coincides with Antonio's misperception: *He* [the Prince] *is enamored on Hero. . . . he swore he would marry her tonight* (2.1.142–148). The much ado about *noting* here prepares for the greater misperceptions to come.

And take her hearing prisoner with the force
And strong encounter° of my amorous tale. *onslaught*
Then after to her father will I break,° *i.e., tell the truth*
And the conclusion is, she shall be thine.[1]
In practice let us put it presently. *They exit.*

1 *As the events stamps them, but they have a good cover; they show well outward.*

The outcome will confirm whether it is good or bad, but it looks good for now.

2 *thick-pleached alley*

Outdoor path lined with trees whose branches intertwine forming an arch

3 *take the present time by the top*

Take advantage of the opportunity. Fortune (or Occasion) was often portrayed as an old woman with a single tuft of hair on the top of her head available to be seized.

Act 1, Scene 2

Enter **Leonato** *and* [**Antonio**].

Leonato

How now, brother. Where is my cousin,° your son? Hath he provided this music?

cousin: kinsman (i.e., nephew)

Antonio

He is very busy about it. But, brother, I can tell you strange news that you yet dreamt not of.

Leonato

Are they° good?

they: i.e., the news

Antonio

As the events° stamps them, but they have a good cover; they show well outward.[1] The Prince and Count Claudio, walking in a thick-pleached alley[2] in mine orchard,° were thus much overheard by a man° of mine: the Prince discovered° to Claudio that he loved my niece your daughter and meant to acknowledge it this night in a dance, and, if he found her accordant,° he meant to take the present time by the top[3] and instantly break° with you of it.

events: outcome / orchard: garden / man: servant / discovered: revealed / accordant: agreeable / break: speak

Leonato

Hath the fellow any wit° that told you this?

wit: intelligence

Antonio

A good sharp fellow. I will send for him, and question him yourself.

Leonato

No, no. We will hold it as a dream till it appear itself. But I will acquaint my daughter withal,° that she may be the better prepared for an answer if peradventure° this be true. Go you and tell her of it.

withal: i.e., with this news / peradventure: by chance

1 *Cousins*

Perhaps *cousins* should be singular, refering to the nephew mentioned in the first line of the scene (although both the Quarto and Folio print *Cousins*). If the plural is indeed correct, it suggests that the bustling entrance includes a number of family members.

2 *I cry you mercy*

I beg your pardon. Perhaps Leonato has bumped into one of the people who has just entered.

3 *have a care*

Be careful

[*Enter kinsmen and attendants.*]

Cousins,[1] you know what you have to do.—Oh, I cry you mercy,[2] friend. Go you with me and I will use your skill.—Good cousin, have a care[3] this busy time. *They exit.*

1 *What the goodyear*

An exclamation of obscure origin; similar to "What the devil"

2 *out of measure*

So extremely

3 *There is no measure in the occasion that breeds*

There is no limit to the situation that causes (my sadness).

4 *born under Saturn*

Born under the influence of the planet Saturn, and therefore "saturnine," or melancholy

5 *mortifying mischief*

Deadly misfortune (i.e., his defeat and, more generally, the disadvantages that come from his bastardy)

6 *I cannot hide what I am.*

(See LONGER NOTE on page 301.)

7 *stood out*

Rebelled

Act 1, Scene 3

*Enter [**Don**] **John** and **Conrade**, his companion.*

Conrade

What the goodyear,[1] my lord! Why are you thus out of measure[2] sad?

Don John

There is no measure in the occasion that breeds,[3] therefore the sadness is without limit.

Conrade

You should hear reason.

Don John

And when I have heard it, what blessing brings it?

Conrade

immediate If not a present° remedy, at least a patient sufferance.

Don John

I wonder that thou, being, as thou say'st thou art, born under Saturn,[4] goest about to apply a moral med'cine to a mortifying mischief.[5] I cannot hide what I am.[6] I must be sad when I have cause and smile at no man's jests, eat when I have stomach° (*appetite*) and wait for no man's leisure, sleep when I am drowsy and tend° (*attend*) on no man's business, laugh when I am merry and claw° no man in his humor.° (*flatter / mood*)

Conrade

Yea, but you must not make the full show of this till you may do it without controlment.° (*restraint*) You have of late stood out[7] against your brother, and he hath ta'en° (*i.e., taken*) you newly into his grace,° (*favor*) where it is impossible you should take true root but by the fair weather that you make yourself. It is needful that you frame° (*shape; fashion*) the season for your own harvest.

1 *I had rather be a canker in a hedge than a rose in his grace*

I.e., I would rather be less well off and independent than thrive with his support. Don John identifies himself with the hardiness of the wild rose (*canker*) rather than the delicacy of the cultivated *rose* that thrives in the court. *Canker*, however, also means (1) a caterpillar or grub that destroys the buds of plants and (2) a spreading sore or ulcer.

2 *fashion a carriage*

Affect a false manner

3 *I am trusted with a muzzle and enfranchised with a clog*

I am trusted as much as an animal that has to wear a *muzzle* or a *clog* (a large block of wood attached to the leg to prevent its escape).

4 *had my mouth*

Were unmuzzled

5 *I make all use of it, for I use it only.*

I.e., I make great use of it, for it is my only resource.

6 **Borachio**

From the Spanish for "wine bottle"; the name designates a drunkard.

7 *What is he for a fool that betroths himself to unquietness?*

What kind of fool is he who weds himself to a life of trouble?

8 *Marry*

Indeed. Deriving from *the Virgin Mary*, the word has been in use as a mild oath since the 14th century, as also in line 47 and elsewhere.

Don John

wild rose I had rather be a canker° in a hedge than a rose in his
disposition / by grace,[1] and it better fits my blood° to be disdained of°
all than to fashion a carriage[2] to rob love from any. In
this, though I cannot be said to be a flattering honest
man, it must not be denied but I am a plain-dealing
villain. I am trusted with a muzzle and enfranchised
resolved with a clog;[3] therefore I have decreed° not to sing in
my cage. If I had my mouth,[4] I would bite; if I had my
liberty, I would do my liking. In the meantime, let me
be that I am and seek not to alter me.

Conrade

Can you make no use of your discontent?

Don John

I make all use of it, for I use it only.[5] Who comes here?

Enter **Borachio**.[6]

What news, Borachio?

Borachio

lavish I came yonder from a great° supper. The Prince your
brother is royally entertained by Leonato, and I can
news give you intelligence° of an intended marriage.

Don John

design Will it serve for any model° to build mischief on?
What is he for a fool that betroths himself to
unquietness?[7]

Borachio

Marry,[8] it is your brother's right hand.

Don John

Who? The most exquisite Claudio?

Borachio

Even he.

1 *A proper squire.*

A fine young man (sarcastic)

2 *March-chick*

I.e., precocious girl (a *March-chick* is one born early in the year)

3 *entertained for a perfumer*

Employed to perfume the rooms of the house (with smoke from burned herbs)

4 *comes me*

Here, and in line 50, *me* is a colloquial form often identified as the ethical dative, which functions mainly to draw attention to the speaker.

5 *cross*

Thwart or vex (but Don John plays on the sense "make the sign of the cross," when he says that it will be to *bless* himself)

6 *o' my mind*

I.e., disposed to poison the food

Don John

A proper squire.[1] And who, and who? Which way looks he?

Borachio

Marry, on Hero, the daughter and heir of Leonato.

Don John

A very forward March-chick![2] How came you to this?

Borachio

perfuming Being entertained for a perfumer,[3] as I was smoking° a musty room, comes me[4] the Prince and Claudio, *serious* hand in hand in sad° conference. I whipped me *wall hanging* behind the arras,° and there heard it agreed upon that the Prince should woo Hero for himself, and, having obtained her, give her to Count Claudio.

Don John

Come; come. Let us thither. This may prove food to *malice / upstart* my displeasure.° That young start-up° hath all the glory of my overthrow. If I can cross[5] him any way, *trustworthy* I bless myself every way. You are both sure° and will assist me?

Conrade

To the death, my lord.

Don John

Let us to the great supper. Their cheer is the greater *because* that° I am subdued. Would the cook were o' my mind![6] *find out* Shall we go prove° what's to be done?

Borachio

attend We'll wait° upon your Lordship. *[They] exit.*

1 **Antonio**

(See Longer Note on page 301).

2 *I am heartburned*

I.e., I get indigestion (from Don John's sour face).

3 *my lady's eldest son*

I.e., a spoiled boy

4 *curst*

Ill-tempered and sharp tongued (usually applied only to women)

Act 2, Scene 1

Enter **Leonato**, [**Antonio**] [1] *(his brother)*, [**Innogen**] *(his wife)*, **Hero** *(his daughter)*, *and* **Beatrice** *(his niece)*.

Leonato

Was not Count John here at supper?

Antonio

I saw him not.

Beatrice

sour How tartly° that gentleman looks! I never can see him but I am heartburned [2] an hour after.

Hero

He is of a very melancholy disposition.

Beatrice

would be He were° an excellent man that were made just in the midway between him and Benedick. The one is too *portrait; statue* like an image° and says nothing, and the other too *chattering* like my lady's eldest son, [3] evermore tattling.°

Leonato

Then half Signior Benedick's tongue in Count John's mouth, and half Count John's melancholy in Signior Benedick's face—

Beatrice

With a good leg and a good foot, uncle, and money enough in his purse, such a man would win any *he* woman in the world, if 'a° could get her good will.

Leonato

By my troth, niece, thou wilt never get thee a husband *critical; shrewish* if thou be so shrewd° of thy tongue.

Antonio

In faith, she's too curst. [4]

1 *God sends a curst cow short horns*

Proverbial: God gives an aggressive (*curst*) cow *short horns* (to keep her from injuring others).

2 *no husband*

I.e., no husband to cuckold

3 *lie in the woolen*

Sleep wrapped in coarse wool blankets

4 *waiting gentlewoman*

An aristocratic woman who serves a woman of higher rank

5 *Therefore I will even take sixpence in earnest of the bearherd and lead his apes into Hell.*

I will take sixpence as a down payment from the *bearherd* (trainer of animals for popular entertainments) and *lead his apes into Hell* (the proverbial fate of unmarried women).

6 *Saint Peter*

Peter traditionally greets souls at the gates of Heaven.

7 *For the heavens*

As for my fate in Heaven (though could possibly be a mild oath or even a designation of Saint Peter's location at the gate, with *For* a variant of "Fore" meaning "in front of").

Beatrice

gift

Too curst is more than curst. I shall lessen God's sending° that way, for it is said, "God sends a curst cow short horns,"[1] but to a cow too curst, he sends none.

Leonato

So, by being too curst, God will send you no horns.

Beatrice

Precisely

Just,° if he send me no husband,[2] for the which blessing I am at him upon my knees every morning and evening. Lord, I could not endure a husband with a beard on his face! I had rather lie in the woolen.[3]

Leonato

settle; alight

You may light° on a husband that hath no beard.

Beatrice

What should I do with him? Dress him in my apparel and make him my waiting gentlewoman?[4] He that hath a beard is more than a youth, and he that hath no beard is less than a man; and he that is more than a youth is not for me, and he that is less than a man, I am not for him. Therefore I will even take sixpence in earnest of the bearherd and lead his apes into Hell.[5]

Leonato

Well then, go you into Hell?

Beatrice

only

unmarried people

No, but° to the gate, and there will the devil meet me like an old cuckold with horns on his head, and say, "Get you to Heaven, Beatrice; get you to Heaven. Here's no place for you maids." So deliver I up my apes and away to Saint Peter.[6] For the heavens,[7] he shows me where the bachelors° sit, and there live we as merry as the day is long.

1 *piece of valiant dust*

I.e., man; Adam, the progenitor of all men, was supposed to have been made from "the dust of the ground" (Genesis 2:7).

2 *clod of wayward marl*

Clump of sinful earth (i.e., a fallen man)

3 *to match in my kindred*

To commit incest by marrying my relative. *The Book of Common Prayer* included a table "of Kindred and Affinity" that listed the relatives that were considered too close to marry.

4 *in that kind*

I.e., with respect to marriage

5 *in good time*

At the right moment (with a musical sense: "in the proper rhythm")

6 *measure*

moderation (but punning on *measure* as a formal, deliberate dance; see line 67)

7 *cinquepace*

A fast-paced, five-step dance (pronounced sink-a-pace, hence the joke at line 69)

8 *full as fantastical*

As fully extravagant

9 *Repentance*

A personification of the anticipated repenting of sin at the end of one's life

Antonio

[*to* **Hero**] Well, niece, I trust you will be ruled by your father.

Beatrice

Yes, faith, it is my cousin's duty to make curtsy and say, "Father, as it please you." But yet for all that, cousin, let him be a handsome fellow, or else make another curtsy and say, "Father, as it please me."

Leonato

[*to* **Beatrice**] Well, niece, I hope to see you one day fitted with a husband.

Beatrice

substance / *by*

Not till God make men of some other metal° than earth. Would it not grieve a woman to be overmastered with° a piece of valiant dust?[1] To make an account of her life to a clod of wayward marl?[2] No, uncle, I'll none. Adam's sons are my brethren, and truly I hold it a sin to match in my kindred.[3]

Leonato

[*to* **Hero**] Daughter, remember what I told you. If the Prince do solicit you in that kind,[4] you know your answer.

Beatrice

overbearing / *courtship* / *properly* / *pomp / dignity*

The fault will be in the music, cousin, if you be not wooed in good time.[5] If the Prince be too important,° tell him there is measure[6] in everything, and so dance out the answer. For hear me, Hero, wooing, wedding, and repenting is as a Scotch jig, a measure, and a cinquepace.[7] The first suit° is hot and hasty like a Scotch jig, and full as fantastical;[8] the wedding, mannerly° modest as a measure, full of state° and ancientry;° and then comes Repentance,[9] and with his bad legs falls into the cinquepace faster and faster till he sink into his grave.

1 *I can see a church by daylight*

I.e., can see what is obvious (the church would be the town's most conspicuous building).

2 *Make good room.*

Give them space; get out of the way.

3 *walk a bout*

I.e., take a turn (though an audience inevitably hears *walk* "about," i.e., around)

4 *God defend the lute should be like the case*

I.e., God forbid your face should be as ugly as your mask.

5 *Philemon's roof*

In classical mythology, Philemon and Baucis entertained a disguised *Jove* (king of the gods) and his son Mercury, the messenger god, in their humble cottage. In return for the peasants' generosity, the gods transformed their modest home into a palace.

6 *thatched*

I.e., like the roofing of *Philemon's* cottage; Hero's point seems to be that Don Pedro's mask should have a moustache and beard.

Leonato

understand / surpassingly Cousin, you apprehend° passing° shrewdly.

Beatrice

I have a good eye, uncle; I can see a church by daylight.[1]

Leonato

The revelers are entering, brother. Make good room.[2]

Enter [**Don**] **Pedro, Claudio, Benedick, Balthasar,** [**Don**] **John,** [**Borachio, Margaret, Ursula,** *and others, masked. Music plays*].

Don Pedro

[*to* **Hero**] Lady, will you walk a bout[3] with your friend?

[*They dance.*]

Hero

As long as So° you walk softly, and look sweetly, and say nothing, I am yours for the walk, and especially when I walk away.

Don Pedro

With me in your company?

Hero

I may say so when I please.

Don Pedro

And when please you to say so?

Hero

face When I like your favor,° for God defend the lute should be like the case![4]

Don Pedro

My visor is Philemon's roof;[5] within the house is Jove.

Hero

mask Why, then, your visor° should be thatched.[6]

1 **Benedick**

Though both the Quarto and Folio assign the speeches beginning at lines 85, 88, and 90 to Benedick, editors often reassign them to Balthasar, because he appears to finish the exchange at line 95, or to Borachio, Margaret's lover. Emendation seems unnecessary, however, since the masquerade consists of brief and playful flirtations not inappropriate for Benedick, and, indeed, Benedick flirts again with Margaret in 5.2.

2 *Answer, clerk.*

I.e., say *Amen* again. It was the parish clerk's duty to lead the responses in church services.

3 *The clerk is answered.*

I.e., I get the message (that you are not interested in me).

Don Pedro

Speak low if you speak love.

[They move aside. **Margaret** *and* **Benedick** *come forward.]*

Benedick[1]

wish Well, I would° you did like me.

Margaret

bad So would not I for your own sake, for I have many ill° qualities.

Benedick

Which is one?

Margaret

I say my prayers aloud.

Benedick

I love you the better; the hearers may cry "Amen."

Margaret

God match me with a good dancer!

*[***Benedick** *moves aside, as* **Balthasar** *comes forward.]*

Balthasar

Amen.

Margaret

And God keep him out of my sight when the dance is done! Answer, clerk.[2]

Balthasar

No more words. The clerk is answered.[3]

[They move aside. **Ursula** *and* **Antonio** *come forward.]*

Ursula

I know you well enough. You are Signior Antonio.

Antonio

In At° a word, I am not.

1 *do him so ill-well*

Imitate his infirmities so well

2 *up and down*

Exactly; in every respect

3 *Go to*

Expression of impatience or disbelief

4 *there's an end*

I.e., that's that.

5 The Hundred Merry Tales

A popular collection of comic stories, first published in 1526

Ursula

I know you by the waggling of your head.

Antonio

To tell you true, I counterfeit him.

Ursula

You could never do him so ill-well[1] unless you were the very man. Here's his dry hand up and down.[2] You are he; you are he.

Antonio

In At° a word, I am not.

Ursula

Come, come, do you think I do not know you by

excellence your excellent wit? Can virtue° hide itself? Go to;[3]

be quiet / Virtues mum.° You are he. Graces° will appear, and there's an end.[4] [*They move aside.* **Beatrice** *and* **Benedick** *come forward.*]

Beatrice

Will you not tell me who told you so?

Benedick

No, you shall pardon me.

Beatrice

Nor will you not tell me who you are?

Benedick

Not now.

Beatrice

That I was disdainful and that I had my good wit out of *The Hundred Merry Tales!*[5] Well this was Signior Benedick that said so.

Benedick

What's he?

1 *only his gift*

His only talent

2 *libertines*

People of loose morals

3 *boarded*

Accosted; approached (literally "come aboard," as on a ship, punning on *fleet*), perhaps so that she could return his insults. Beatrice may also suggest that she wishes Benedick would woo her.

4 *break a comparison or two*

Hit me with one or two (slanderous but ineffective) comparisons (like a lance that breaks in joust).

5 *peradventure not marked*

By chance not noticed

6 *partridge wing*

Partridge wings were considered delicious but recognized for having very little meat on them.

Beatrice

I am sure you know him well enough.

Benedick

Not I, believe me.

Beatrice

Did he never make you laugh?

Benedick

I pray you, what is he?

Beatrice

Why, he is the Prince's jester, a very dull fool, only his gift[1] is in devising impossible° slanders. None but libertines[2] delight in him, and the commendation is not in his wit but in his villainy,° for he both pleases men and angers them, and then they laugh at him and beat him. I am sure he is in the fleet.° I would he had boarded[3] me.

outrageous

rudeness

group of dancers

Benedick

When I know° the gentleman, I'll tell him what you say.

i.e., meet

Beatrice

Do; do. He'll but break a comparison or two[4] on me, which peradventure not marked[5] or not laughed at strikes him into melancholy, and then there's a partridge wing[6] saved, for the fool will eat no supper that night. We must follow° the leaders. [*They join the dance.*]

(in the dance)

Benedick

In every good thing.

Beatrice

Nay, if they lead to any ill, I will leave them at the next turning.°

change in formation

1 *amorous on*

In love with (like *enamored on* in line 143)

2 *these ill news*

This bad news (*News* was commonly treated as a plural noun, as in 1.2.4.)

Dance, [then] they [all] exit [except **Don John**, **Borachio**, *and* **Claudio**].

Don John

Surely *speak* *i.e., masked person*

Sure° my brother is amorous on[1] Hero and hath withdrawn her father to break° with him about it. The ladies follow her, and but one visor° remains.

Borachio

And that is Claudio; I know him by his bearing.

Don John

[*to* **Claudio**] Are not you Signior Benedick?

Claudio

You know me well; I am he.

Don John

favor *social rank*

Signior, you are very near my brother in his love.° He is enamored on Hero. I pray you, dissuade him from her. She is no equal for his birth.° You may do the part of an honest man in it.

Claudio

How know you he loves her?

Don John

I heard him swear his affection.

Borachio

So did I too, and he swore he would marry her tonight.

Don John

i.e., dessert

Come; let us to the banquet.°

[**Don John** *and* **Borachio**] *exit.* **Claudio** *remains.*

Claudio

Thus answer I in name of Benedick,
But hear these ill news[2] with the ears of Claudio.

1 *This is an accident of hourly proof*

I.e., such betrayals can be seen every hour.

2 *willow*

The willow tree was a traditional symbol of unrequited love.

3 *What fashion will you wear the garland of?*

How will you wear your willow garland?

4 *an usurer's chain*

A large gold chain often worn by moneylenders

5 *so they sell bullocks*

I.e., cattle dealers confirm their sales with such words as "I wish you joy of her."

certainly 'Tis certain° so: the Prince woos for himself.
Friendship is constant in all other things
Except / business Save° in the office° and affairs of love.
let all Therefore all° hearts in love use their own tongues.
Let every eye negotiate for itself
And trust no agent, for beauty is a witch
loyalty / passion Against whose charms faith° melteth into blood.°
This is an accident of hourly proof,[1]
suspected Which I mistrusted° not. Farewell, therefore, Hero.

Enter **Benedick**.

Benedick
Count Claudio?

Claudio
Yea, the same.

Benedick
Come; will you go with me?

Claudio
Where Whither?°

Benedick
Even to the next willow,[2] about your own business, *Count* County.° What fashion will you wear the garland of?[3] About your neck like an usurer's chain?[4] Or under your *sash / some* arm like a lieutenant's scarf?° You must wear it one° way, for the Prince hath got your Hero.

Claudio
I wish him joy of her.

Benedick
cattle dealer Why, that's spoken like an honest drover;° so they sell bullocks.[5] But did you think the Prince would have served you thus?

1 *now you strike like the blind man. 'Twas the boy that stole your meat, and you'll beat the post.*

I.e., you are shooting at the messenger, like the blind man who beat a pillar (*post*, playing on both its senses: "pillar" and "messenger") instead of the boy who stole his meat.

2 *If it will not be*

I.e., if you will not *leave* me

3 *poor hurt fowl, now will he creep into sedges*

Poor injured bird, now he will hide himself among reeds (in order to allow his wounds to heal).

4 *but so I am apt to do myself wrong*

I.e., but if I accept the idea that I am considered *the Prince's fool*, then I slander myself.

5 *It is the base, though bitter, disposition of Beatrice that puts the world into her person and so gives me out.*

It is Beatrice's ungenerous but biting nature that makes her believe everyone thinks as harshly as she does, and so she describes me (*gives me out*) as if she speaks for the whole world.

6 *a lodge in a warren*

Perhaps, a gamekeeper's lodging in a game park, which would be simple and isolated. There is some disagreement about the precise sense of this line, though the simile is obviously meant to convey just how melancholy Claudio is.

Claudio

I pray you, leave me.

Benedick

Ho, now you strike like the blind man. 'Twas the boy that stole your meat, and you'll beat the post.[1]

Claudio

If it will not be,[2] I'll leave you. *He exits.*

Benedick

Alas, poor hurt fowl, now will he creep into sedges.[3] But that my Lady Beatrice should know me, and not know me! The Prince's fool? Ha! It may be I go under that title because I am merry. Yea, but so I am apt to do myself wrong.[4] I am not so reputed! It is the base, though bitter, disposition of Beatrice that puts the world into her person and so gives me out.[5] Well, I'll be revenged as I may.

Enter [**Don Pedro**], **Hero**, *and* **Leonato**.

Don Pedro

Now, signior, where's the Count? Did you see him?

Benedick

Rumor

Troth, my lord, I have played the part of Lady Fame.° I found him here as melancholy as a lodge in a warren.[6] I told him, and I think I told him true, that your Grace had got the good will of this young lady, and I offered him my company to a willow tree, either to make him a garland, as being forsaken, or to bind him up a rod,° as being worthy to be whipped.

bundle of twigs

Don Pedro

To be whipped? What's his fault?

1 *Wilt thou make a trust a transgression?*

I.e., do you think that trust is an error?

2 *Yet it had not been amiss the rod had been made*

But it would not have been wrong to prepare a rod (for punishment); see line 192.

3 *If their singing answer your saying, by my faith, you say honestly.*

If their song confirms what you have said, then truly you are acting in good faith.

4 *past the endurance of a block*

More than even an insensible object could stand

5 *but with one green leaf on it*

I.e., with only the slightest sign of life

6 *duller than a great thaw*

I.e., more boring than the late winter (when melting ice and snow make the roads too muddy for travel and everyone stays indoors)

7 *imposssible conveyance*

Incredible skill

Benedick

The flat° transgression of a schoolboy, who, being over-joyed with finding a birds' nest, shows it° his companion, and he steals it.

basic
it to

Don Pedro

Wilt thou make a trust a transgression?[1] The transgression is in the stealer.

Benedick

Yet it had not been amiss the rod had been made,[2] and the garland too, for the garland he might have worn himself and the rod he might have bestowed° on you, who, as I take it, have stolen his birds' nest.

i.e., used

Don Pedro

I will but teach them to sing and restore them to the owner.

Benedick

If their singing answer your saying, by my faith, you say honestly.[3]

Don Pedro

The Lady Beatrice hath a quarrel to° you. The gentleman that danced with her told her she is much wronged by you.

with

Benedick

Oh, she misused° me past the endurance of a block.[4] An oak but with one green leaf on it[5] would have answered her. My very visor° began to assume life and scold° with her. She told me, not thinking I had been myself, that I was the Prince's jester, that I was duller than a great thaw,[6] huddling° jest upon jest with such impossible conveyance[7] upon me that I stood like a man at a mark° with a whole army shooting at me.

abused
mask
quarrel
piling up
target

1 *to the North Star*

I.e., everything between her and the North Star

2 *all that Adam had left him before he transgressed*

I.e., all the pleasures Adam enjoyed in the Garden of Eden before the Fall

3 *She would have made Hercules have turned spit, yea, and have cleft his club to make the fire, too.*

She would emasculate even Hercules, making him perform such domestic chores as turning the roasting spit, and furthermore she would have broken his massive club and used it to make the fire.

4 *infernal Ate*

The hellish goddess of discord (pronounced Ah-tay), daughter of Zeus

5 *I would to God some scholar would conjure her, for, certainly, while she is here, a man may live as quiet in Hell as in a sanctuary, and people sin upon purpose because they would go thither.*

I wish some scholar would send her back to Hell, for while she is here on Earth, Hell is a quiet refuge, and people sin intentionally so that they can go there.

6 *I will go on the slightest errand now to the Antipodes that you can devise to send me on. I will fetch you a toothpicker now from the furthest inch of Asia, bring you the length of Prester John's foot, fetch you a hair off the great Cham's beard, do you any embassage to the Pygmies*

All these places and characters exist at what Benedick imagines to be *the world's end*: the *Antipodes* was the region on the opposite side of the globe; *Prester John* was a legendary Christian priest and ruler of a region in the Middle East; the *great Cham* is Kublai Khan (or possibly Genghis Khan), who ruled Mongolia; the *Pygmies* were a race of diminutive people thought to dwell in Ethiopia or India. His point is that he will do anything at all to get away from her.

7 *harpy*

Wicked mythical creature, half woman and half bird of prey, known for its savageness

She speaks poniards,° and every word stabs. If her breath were as terrible as her terminations,° there were no living near her; she would infect to the North Star.[1] I would not marry her though° she were endowed with all that Adam had left him before he transgressed.[2] She would have made Hercules have turned spit, yea, and have cleft° his club to make the fire, too.[3] Come; talk not of her. You shall find her the infernal Ate[4] in good apparel. I would to God some scholar would conjure her, for, certainly, while she is here,° a man may live as quiet in Hell as in a sanctuary, and people sin upon purpose because they would go thither.[5] So indeed all disquiet, horror, and perturbation follows° her.

poniards: daggers; terminations: descriptive terms; though: even if; cleft: split; here: i.e., on Earth; follows: waits on

Enter **Claudio** *and* **Beatrice**.

Don Pedro

Look. Here she comes.

Benedick

Will your Grace command me any service to the world's end? I will go on the slightest errand now to the Antipodes that you can devise to send me on. I will fetch you a toothpicker° now from the furthest inch of Asia, bring you the length of Prester John's foot, fetch you a hair off the great Cham's beard, do you any embassage to the Pygmies,[6] rather than hold three words' conference with this harpy.[7] You have no employment for me?

toothpicker: toothpick

Don Pedro

None but to desire your good company.

1 *Indeed, my lord, he lent it me awhile, and I gave him use for it: a double heart for his single one. Marry, once before he won it of me with false dice. Therefore your Grace may well say I have lost it.*

The passage, suggesting a previous failed relationship between Benedick and Beatrice, has provided recent actresses with motivation for the role. Judi Dench (1976), for example, took her cue for the role from these lines, reciting them with a "flicker of pain"; "you felt her wit was a defence against further breakages." So, likewise to varying degrees, Sinead Cusack (1982–1985), Samantha Bond (1988), and Emma Thompson (1993) (see Cox in For Further Reading).

2 *put him down*

Humiliated him. Beatrice's reply gives the phrase *put him down* a sexual connotation: if Benedick put her down (i.e., took her to bed) she would give birth to fools.

3 *civil as an orange*

A pun on *civil* meaning "somber" and *Seville*, a town in Spain famous for its bittersweet oranges

4 *jealous complexion*

I.e., yellow coloring; yellow was associated with jealousy.

Benedick

O God, sir, here's a dish I love not. I cannot endure my Lady Tongue! *He exits.*

Don Pedro

[*to* **Beatrice**] Come, lady, come. You have lost the heart of Signior Benedick.

Beatrice

Indeed, my lord, he lent it me awhile, and I gave him use° for it: a double heart for his single one. Marry, once before he won it of° me with false dice. Therefore your Grace may well say I have lost it.[1]

interest · *from*

Don Pedro

You have put him down,[2] lady; you have put him down.

Beatrice

So I would not he should do me, my lord, lest I should prove the mother of fools. I have brought Count Claudio, whom you sent me to seek.

Don Pedro

Why, how now, Count? Wherefore° are you sad?

Why

Claudio

Not sad, my lord.

Don Pedro

How then? Sick?

Claudio

Neither, my lord.

Beatrice

The Count is neither sad, nor sick, nor merry, nor well, but civil° Count, civil as an orange,[3] and something of that jealous complexion.[4]

somber

1 *His Grace hath made the match, and all grace say "Amen" to it.*

Don Pedro has made the match, and may Heaven bless it.

2 *poor fool*

Referring deprecatingly to her *merry heart*

3 *on the windy side of care*

On the windward side of care (and therefore upwind of and thus away from any worries)

4 *Good Lord, for alliance*

Thank God for relatives by marriage; Beatrice comically returns Claudio's greeting of *cousin*.

5 *Thus goes everyone to the world but I*

I.e., so everyone marries but I

6 *sunburnt*

I.e., dark, which was conventionally thought to be unattractive

7 *Heigh-ho for a husband*

Proverbial cry of a single woman seeking a husband, and the title of a popular ballad.

Don Pedro

I' faith, lady, I think your blazon° to be true,° though, I'll be sworn, if he be so, his conceit° is false.—Here, Claudio, I have wooed in thy name, and fair Hero is won. I have broke° with her father and his good will obtained. Name the day of marriage, and God give thee joy.

description / accurate
understanding
spoken

Leonato

Count, take of me my daughter, and with her my fortunes. His Grace hath made the match, and all grace say "Amen" to it.[1]

Beatrice

Speak, Count; 'tis your cue.

Claudio

Silence is the perfectest herald° of joy. I were but little happy if I could say how much.—Lady, as you are mine, I am yours. I give away myself for you and dote upon the exchange.

i.e., expression

Beatrice

Speak, cousin, or, if you cannot, stop his mouth with a kiss and let not him speak neither.

Don Pedro

In faith, lady, you have a merry heart.

Beatrice

Yea, my lord. I thank it, poor fool;[2] it keeps° on the windy side of care.[3] My cousin tells him in his ear that he is in her heart.

stays

Claudio

And so she doth, cousin.

Beatrice

Good Lord, for alliance![4] Thus goes everyone to the world but I,[5] and I am sunburnt.[6] I may sit in a corner and cry, "Heigh-ho for a husband!"[7]

1 *come by*

Acquire

2 *out o' question*

Without a doubt

3 *a star danced*

I.e., a shooting star (though perhaps the reference is to the idea that the sun danced on Easter Sunday), which influenced her temperament; see 1.3.9 and note.

4 *cry you mercy*

Beg your pardon

5 *melancholy element*

The humor that causes melancholy; see 1.1.113 and note.

Don Pedro

Lady Beatrice, I will get you one.

Beatrice

I would rather have one of your father's getting.° Hath your Grace ne'er° a brother like you? Your father got° excellent husbands, if a maid could come by[1] them.

begetting
not / begot

Don Pedro

Will you have me, lady?

Beatrice

No, my lord, unless I might have another for working days. Your Grace is too costly to wear every day. But I beseech your Grace pardon me. I was born to speak all mirth and no matter.°

substance

Don Pedro

Your silence most offends me, and to be merry best becomes you, for out o' question[2] you were born in a merry hour.

Beatrice

No, sure,° my lord. My mother cried, but then there was a star danced,[3] and under that was I born.—Cousins, God give you joy!

surely

Leonato

Niece, will you look to those things I told you of?

Beatrice

I cry you mercy,[4] uncle.—By your Grace's pardon.

Beatrice exits.

Don Pedro

By my troth, a pleasant-spirited lady.

Leonato

There's little of the melancholy element[5] in her, my

1 *Monday, my dear son, which is hence a just sevennight*

This helps establish the time scheme of the play: the soldiers arrive on Monday (2.1) and the wedding (4.1) is set for the following Monday (*a just sevennight*, i.e., exactly a week). The second eavesdropping scene (3.1) takes place just before the wedding, so, presumably on Sunday; Claudio and company spy on Hero that night, the night before the wedding. There are some slight indications that Hero's presumed death, Don John's flight, Borachio's confession, and the mourning scene happen also on that fateful wedding Monday, and that the second wedding occurs on the next day, Tuesday. But Shakespeare, as usual, does not concern himself with working out a strict temporal sequence and allows these later events to seem as if they are separated by more time.

2 *Hercules' labors*

In classical mythology, twelve seemingly impossible tasks undertaken by Hercules as a punishment for slaying his family

serious / *always / i.e., Beatrice*

lord. She is never sad° but when she sleeps, and not ever° sad then, for I have heard my daughter say she° hath often dreamt of unhappiness and waked herself with laughing.

Don Pedro

She cannot endure to hear tell of a husband.

Leonato

courting

Oh, by no means. She mocks all her wooers out of suit.°

Don Pedro

would be

She were° an excellent wife for Benedick.

Leonato

O Lord, my lord, if they were but a week married, they would talk themselves mad.

Don Pedro

Count

County° Claudio, when mean you to go to church?

Claudio

Tomorrow, my lord. Time goes on crutches till love have all his rites.

Leonato

conform to / liking

Not till Monday, my dear son, which is hence a just sevennight,[1] and a time too brief, too, to have all things answer° my mind.°

Don Pedro

interval / promise / *eagerly* / *arrange* / *provide*

[*to* **Claudio**] Come; you shake the head at so long a breathing,° but, I warrant° thee, Claudio, the time shall not go dully by us. I will in the interim undertake one of Hercules' labors,[2] which is to bring Signior Benedick and the Lady Beatrice into a mountain of affection, th' one with th' other. I would fain° have it a match, and I doubt not but to fashion° it, if you three will but minister° such assistance as I shall give you direction.

1 *ten nights' watchings*

Ten sleepless nights

2 *modest office*

Seemly act

3 *queasy stomach*

I.e., distaste for marriage

Leonato

behind; in support of My lord, I am for° you, though it cost me ten nights' watchings.[1]

Claudio

And I, my lord.

Don Pedro

And you too, gentle Hero?

Hero

I will do any modest office,[2] my lord, to help my cousin to a good husband.

Don Pedro

least promising And Benedick is not the unhopefullest° husband that I know. Thus far can I praise him: he is of a noble *lineage / proven / honor* strain,° of approved° valor, and confirmed honesty.° I will teach you how to humor your cousin that she shall fall in love with Benedick, and I, with your two *work (my schemes)* helps, will so practice° on Benedick that, in despite of his quick wit and his queasy stomach,[3] he shall fall in love with Beatrice. If we can do this, Cupid is no longer an archer; his glory shall be ours, for we are the only *plan* love gods. Go in with me, and I will tell you my drift.°

[They] exit.

1 *whatsoever comes athwart his affection ranges evenly with mine*

Whatever frustrates his desires fits perfectly with my own.

2 *Margaret, the waiting gentlewoman to Hero*

(See **Longer Note, page 302)**

3 *unseasonable instant*

Inappropriate hour

Act 2, Scene 2

Enter [**Don**] **John** *and* **Borachio**.

Don John

It is so. The Count Claudio shall marry the daughter of Leonato.

Borachio

thwart; block

Yea, my lord, but I can cross° it.

Don John

obstacle / *with*

Any bar,° any cross, any impediment will be med'cinable to me. I am sick in displeasure to° him, and whatsoever comes athwart his affection ranges evenly with mine.[1] How canst thou cross this marriage?

Borachio

Not honestly, my lord, but so covertly that no dishonesty shall appear in me.

Don John

Show me briefly how.

Borachio

ago

I think I told your Lordship a year since° how much I am in the favor of Margaret, the waiting gentlewoman to Hero.[2]

Don John

I remember.

Borachio

arrange with / bedroom

I can, at any unseasonable instant[3] of the night, appoint° her to look out at her lady's chamber° window.

Don John

What life is in that to be the death of this marriage?

Borachio

with / concoct / *Hesitate*

The poison of that lies in° you to temper.° Go you to the Prince your brother. Spare° not to tell him that he hath wronged his honor in marrying the renowned Claudio,

1 *Only to despite*

Purely to torment

2 *is thus like to be cozened with the semblance of a maid*

Is about to be betrayed by a woman who is a virgin in appearance only

3 *"Claudio"*

Some editors believe this to be an error and substitute "Borachio," but others keep the Quarto and Folio reading (as here), arguing that Borachio intends to invite Margaret to play a lascivious game in which they will pretend to be their social superiors, and which will force Claudio to think he sees Hero wooing another man and mocking him by using his name. In this version of the plot, Margaret does not have to suspect any wrongdoing.

4 *preparation*

i.e., for the wedding

5 *Grow this to what adverse issue it can*

Let this produce the most harmful outcome possible.

reputation; worth *prostitute*

whose estimation° do you mightily hold up, to a contaminated stale,° such a one as Hero.

Don John

What proof shall I make of that?

Borachio

delude / torture *ruin* *outcome*

Proof enough to misuse° the Prince, to vex° Claudio, to undo° Hero, and kill Leonato. Look you for any other issue?°

Don John

Only to despite[1] them, I will endeavor anything.

Borachio

suitable *Pretend* *for* *revealed* *evidence* *suspicion / certainty*

Go then. Find me a meet° hour to draw Don Pedro and the Count Claudio alone. Tell them that you know that Hero loves me. Intend° a kind of zeal both to the Prince and Claudio, as in° love of your brother's honor, who hath made this match, and his friend's reputation, who is thus like to be cozened with the semblance of a maid,[2] that you have discovered° thus. They will scarcely believe this without trial. Offer them instances,° which shall bear no less likelihood than to see me at her chamber window, hear me call Margaret "Hero," hear Margaret term me "Claudio,"[3] and bring them to see this the very night before the intended wedding; for in the meantime I will so fashion the matter that Hero shall be absent, and there shall appear such seeming truth of Hero's disloyalty that jealousy° shall be called assurance° and all the preparation[4] overthrown.

Don John

Grow this to what adverse issue it can;[5] I will put it in

practice. Be cunning in the working this, and thy fee is a thousand ducats.°

gold coins

Borachio

Be you constant° in the accusation, and my cunning shall not shame me.

steadfast

Don John

I will presently° go learn their day of marriage.

immediately

[They] exit.

1 *I am here already*

I.e., I will do it right away; Benedick pretends to take him literally.

2 *I have known when there was no music with him but the drum and the fife, and now had he rather hear the tabor and the pipe.*

I remember when his only interest was soldiering, but now he prefers the pleasures of peacetime.

3 *now is he turned orthography*

Now he has turned into a flowery speaker. (*Orthography* is literally the study of correct spelling, but here means "rhetorician.")

Act 2, Scene 3

Enter **Benedick** *alone.*

Benedick

Boy!

[*Enter* **Boy**.]

Boy

Signior?

Benedick

In my chamber window lies a book. Bring it hither to me in the orchard.

Boy

I am here already,[1] sir.

Benedick

I know that, but I would have thee hence and here again.

[**Boy**] *exits.*

I do much wonder that one man, seeing how much another man is a fool when he dedicates his behaviors to love, will, after he hath laughed at such shallow follies in others, become the argument° of his own scorn by falling in love—and such a man is Claudio. I have known when there was no music with him but the drum and the fife, and now had he rather hear the tabor and the pipe.[2] I have known when he would have walked ten mile afoot to see a good armor, and now will he lie ten nights awake carving° the fashion of a new doublet.° He was wont° to speak plain and to the purpose, like an honest man and a soldier, and now is he turned orthography;[3] his words are a very fantastical banquet, just so many strange dishes.

subject

designing

jacket / accustomed

1 *see with these eyes*

I.e., still see

2 *I will not be sworn but love may*

I won't swear that love will not

3 *I'll none*

I'll have none (of her).

4 *not I for an angel*

I would not even if she were an angel. Benedick puns on *angel*, the name of a coin, and also on *noble* (also a coin) earlier in the line.

5 *of good discourse*

Well spoken

6 *The music ended*

Once the music is ended

7 *fit the kid-fox with a pennyworth*

I.e., give Benedick his "just deserts." *Pennyworth* is equivalent to "money's worth," and "to have one's pennyworth" meant "to have revenge on."

May I be so converted and see with these eyes?[1] I cannot tell; I think not. I will not be sworn but love may[2] transform me to an oyster, but, I'll take my oath on it, till he have made an oyster of me, he shall never make me such a fool. One woman is fair, yet I am well;° another is wise, yet I am well; another virtuous, yet I am well; but till all graces be in one woman, one woman shall not come in my grace.° Rich she shall be, that's certain; wise, or I'll none;[3] virtuous, or I'll never cheapen° her; fair, or I'll never look on° her; mild, or come not near me; noble, or not I for an angel;[4] of good discourse,[5] an excellent musician, and her hair shall be—of what color it please God. Ha! The Prince and Monsieur Love! I will hide me in the arbor. [*He hides.*]

content / *favor* / *bargain for* / *at*

Enter [**Don Pedro**], **Leonato**, **Claudio**, [*and* **Balthasar** *with*] *music.*

Don Pedro
Come; shall we hear this music?

Claudio
Yea, my good lord. How still the evening is,
As° hushed on purpose to grace harmony!°

As if / music

Don Pedro
[*aside to* **Claudio**] See you where Benedick hath hid
himself?

Claudio
[*aside to* **Don Pedro**] Oh, very well, my lord. The music
ended,[6]
We'll fit the kid-fox with a pennyworth.[7]

1 *It is the witness still of excellency / To put a strange face on his own perfection.*

It is always evidence of an excellent character when a man pretends not to know his own perfections.

2 *crotchets*

(1) quarter notes; (2) fanciful phrases

3 *Note notes, forsooth, and nothing.*

I.e., get on with it; play your music and nothing else. Lines 52–55 pun on various senses of *note*: (1) a musical note; (2) short comment; (3) pay attention to. Also *nothing* and *noting* were pronounced similarly in Shakespeare's time.

4 *sheeps' guts*

Dried intestines of sheep were used to make instrument strings.

5 *horn*

A military or hunting horn (instead of Balthasar's guitar or lute), but also another allusion to the horn of the cuckold

Don Pedro

Come, Balthasar; we'll hear that song again.

Balthasar

demand Oh, good my lord, tax° not so bad a voice
To slander music any more than once.

Don Pedro

It is the witness still of excellency
To put a strange face on[1] his own perfection.
entreat I pray thee, sing, and let me woo° no more.

Balthasar

Because you talk of wooing, I will sing,
Since many a wooer doth commence his suit
To her he thinks not worthy, yet he woos;
Yet will he swear he loves.

Don Pedro

Nay, pray thee, come,
Or if thou wilt hold longer argument,
music Do it in notes.°

Balthasar

Note this before my notes:
There's not a note of mine that's worth the noting.

Don Pedro

Why, these are very crotchets[2] that he speaks!
Note notes, forsooth, and nothing.[3]

[**Balthasar** *plays.*]

Benedick

captivated [*aside*] Now, divine air! Now is his soul ravished.°
drag Is it not strange that sheeps' guts[4] should hale° souls out of men's bodies? Well, a horn[5] for my money, when all's done.

1 *Sigh no more, ladies, sigh no more, / Men were deceivers ever*

Balthasar's song opposes the larger action of the play by attributing inconstancy and fraud to men not women. Branagh used it three times in his film: once at the opening in Beatrice's "wry, ironic voice," accompanied by a text and bouncing ball to lead the audience into Shakespeare's language and the play; then here "in an idealised garden setting where it appeals to Claudio's high romanticism, and finally at the end where it becomes a hard-won confirmation of a certain reality in the relationships between men and women" (see Branagh in the For Further Reading section). Other songs and dances appear in the language and action of the play: Beatrice's comparison of *wooing, wedding,* and *repenting* to a *Scotch jig, measure,* and *cinquepace* (2.1.63–64) and mention of the ballad, *Heigh-ho for a husband* (2.1.287); the dance in the masquerade scene (2.1.73ff.); Margaret's offer to dance to *Light o' love* (3.4.40) a popular song; the song Benedick sings (5.2.20–23; see note); the song at the monument (5.3.12ff.); the music and dance that end the play (5.4.129ff.).

2 *blithe and bonny*

Happy and beautiful

3 *nonny nonny*

I.e., trifles; nothings

4 *for a shift*

I.e., to get by; in a pinch

5 *night raven*

Thought to be a harbinger of bad tidings

Balthasar

[*singing*] Sigh no more, ladies, sigh no more,
Men were deceivers ever,[1]
One foot in sea and one on shore,
To one thing constant never.
Then sigh not so, but let them go,
And be you blithe and bonny,[2]
Converting all your sounds of woe
Into hey, nonny nonny.[3]
more Sing no more ditties, sing no moe°
sad songs / gloomy Of dumps° so dull° and heavy.
The fraud of men was ever so,
in full leaf Since summer first was leavy.°
Then sigh not so, but let them go,
And be you blithe and bonny,
Converting all your sounds of woe
Into hey, nonny nonny.

Don Pedro

faith By my troth,° a good song.

Balthasar

bad And an ill° singer, my lord.

Don Pedro

Ha! No, no, faith, thou sing'st well enough for a shift.[4]

Benedick

If [*aside*] An° he had been a dog that should have howled thus, they would have hanged him, and I pray God his *gladly* bad voice bode no mischief. I had as lief° have heard *no matter* the night raven,[5] come° what plague could have come after it.

Don Pedro

(a mild oath) Yea, marry,° dost thou hear, Balthasar? I pray thee,

1 *Stalk on; stalk on. The fowl sits.*

Go carefully; the bird is perched (and therefore ready to be caught).

2 *Sits the wind in that corner?*

I.e., does the wind blow that way?; is that how things are?

3 *past the infinite of thought*

Beyond anything that could have been imagined (but true)

4 *Faith, like enough.*

Indeed, that is likely enough.

get us some excellent music, for tomorrow night we would have it at° the lady Hero's chamber window.

played underneath

Balthasar

The best I can, my lord.

Don Pedro

Do so. Farewell. **Balthasar** *exits.*

Come hither, Leonato. What was it you told me of today: that your niece Beatrice was in love with Signior Benedick?

Claudio

Oh, ay. [*aside to* **Don Pedro**] Stalk on; stalk on. The fowl sits.[1] [*allowing* **Benedick** *to hear*]—I did never think that lady would have loved any man.

Leonato

No, nor I neither, but most wonderful that she should so dote on Signior Benedick, whom she hath in all outward behaviors seemed ever to abhor.

Benedick

[*aside*] Is 't possible? Sits the wind in that corner?[2]

Leonato

By my troth, my lord, I cannot tell what to think of it, but that she loves him with an enraged° affection; it is past the infinite of thought.[3]

ardent

Don Pedro

May be she doth but counterfeit.°

pretend

Claudio

Faith, like enough.[4]

Leonato

O God! Counterfeit? There was never counterfeit of passion came so near the life of passion as she discovers° it.

displays

1 *She will sit you*

She will often sit (*you* is the ethical dative, a use of the pronoun to emphasize the hearer's presumed interest).

2 *ta'en th' infection*

I.e., taken the bait

Don Pedro

Why, what effects of passion shows she?

Claudio

[*aside to* **Leonato**] Bait the hook well; this fish will bite.

Leonato

What effects, my lord? She will sit you[1]—you heard my daughter tell you how.

Claudio

She did indeed.

Don Pedro

How? How I pray you? You amaze me. I would have thought her spirit had been invincible against all assaults of affection.

Leonato

I would have sworn it had, my lord, especially against Benedick.

Benedick

hoax/except [*aside*] I should think this a gull° but° that the white-
i.e., Leonato bearded fellow° speaks it. Knavery cannot, sure, hide
itself/respectability himself° in such reverence.°

Claudio

[*aside to* **Don Pedro**] He hath ta'en th' infection;[2]
keep hold° it up.

Don Pedro

Hath she made her affection known to Benedick?

Leonato

No, and swears she never will. That's her torment.

Claudio

'Tis true indeed, so your daughter says. "Shall I," says
i.e., Beatrice she,° "that have so oft encountered him with scorn,
write to him that I love him?"

1 *she found "Benedick" and "Beatrice" between the sheet*

She found the names "Benedick" and "Beatrice" written on the sheet of paper (but with an obvious sexual suggestion).

2 *That.*

Most likely an expression of disappointment that Leonato already knows the joke

Leonato

This says she now when she is beginning to write to him, for she'll be up twenty times a night, and there will she sit in her smock° till she have writ a sheet of paper. My daughter tells us all.

slip

Claudio

Now° you talk of a sheet of paper, I remember a pretty° jest your daughter told us of.

Now that / *witty*

Leonato

Oh, when she° had writ it and was reading it over, she found "Benedick" and "Beatrice" between the sheet?[1]

i.e., Beatrice

Claudio

That.[2]

Leonato

Oh, she tore the letter into a thousand halfpence,° railed at herself that she should be so immodest° to write to one that she knew would flout° her. "I measure him," says she, "by my own spirit, for I should flout him if he writ to me, yea, though I love him, I should."

i.e., little pieces / *forward* / *mock*

Claudio

Then down upon her knees she falls, weeps, sobs, beats her heart, tears her hair, prays, curses: "O sweet Benedick! God give me patience!"

Leonato

She doth indeed—my daughter says so—and the ecstasy° hath so much overborne° her that my daughter is sometime afeared she will do a desperate outrage° to herself. It is very true.

frenzy / overwhelmed / *injury*

Don Pedro

It were good that Benedick knew of it by some other, if she will not discover° it.

reveal

1 *half myself*

I.e., my wife

2 *she will die if he woo her rather than she will bate one breath of her accustomed crossness*

I.e., even if he woos her, she would rather die than hold back the slightest bit of her usual contrariness.

Claudio

To what end? He would make but a sport of it and torment the poor lady worse.

Don Pedro

If / act of charity

An° he should, it were an alms° to hang him. She's an excellent sweet lady, and, out of all suspicion, she is virtuous.

Claudio

And she is exceeding wise.

Don Pedro

In everything but in loving Benedick.

Leonato

passion

O my lord, wisdom and blood° combating in so tender a body, we have ten proofs to one that blood hath the victory. I am sorry for her, as I have just cause being her uncle and her guardian.

Don Pedro

affection
put off / considerations

I would she had bestowed this dotage° on me. I would have doffed° all other respects° and made her half myself.[1] I pray you tell Benedick of it and hear what he will say.

Leonato

Were it good, think you?

Claudio

i.e., Beatrice

Hero thinks surely she° will die, for she says she will die if he love her not, and she will die ere she make her love known, and she will die if he woo her rather than she will bate one breath of her accustomed crossness.[2]

Don Pedro

an offer
contemptuous

She doth well. If she should make tender° of her love, 'tis very possible he'll scorn it, for the man, as you know all, hath a contemptible° spirit.

1 *a good outward happiness*

A handsome appearance

2 *Before God*

I.e., that's true.

3 *Hector*

A prince of Troy who was a hero in the Trojan War before he was slain by Achilles

4 *large*

Coarse; inappropriate

Claudio

He is a very proper° man. *handsome*

Don Pedro

He hath indeed a good outward happiness.[1]

Claudio

Before God,[2] and in my mind, very wise.

Don Pedro

He doth indeed show some sparks that are like wit.

Claudio

And I take him to be valiant.

Don Pedro

As Hector,[3] I assure you, and in the managing of quarrels you may say he is wise, for either he avoids them with great discretion or undertakes them with a most Christian-like fear.

Leonato

If he do fear God, 'a° must necessarily keep peace. If he break the peace, he ought to enter into a quarrel with fear and trembling. *he*

Don Pedro

And so will he do, for the man doth fear God, howsoever it seems not in him by° some large[4] jests he will make. Well, I am sorry for your niece. Shall we go seek Benedick and tell him of her love? *to judge by*

Claudio

Never tell him, my lord; let her wear it out with good counsel.° *advice*

Leonato

Nay, that's impossible. She may wear her heart out first.

Don Pedro

Well, we will hear further of it by° your daughter. Let *from*

1 *the while*

In the meantime

2 *The sport will be when they hold one an opinion of another's dotage, and no such matter.*

The fun part will be when each imagines the other to be in love, when it is not the case.

3 *a dumb show*

A performance without words, such as a pantomime; i.e., Benedick and Beatrice will be uncharacteristically speechless.

4 *have their full bent*

Are fully extended (literally stretched like a fully drawn bowstring)

5 *put them to mending*

Resolve to fix them

it cool the while.[1] I love Benedick well, and I could wish he would modestly examine himself to see how much he is unworthy so good a lady.

Leonato

My lord, will you walk? Dinner is ready.

Claudio

[*aside to* **Don Pedro** *and* **Leonato**] If he do not dote on her upon° this, I will never trust my expectation.°

after / predictions

Don Pedro

[*aside to* **Leonato**] Let there be the same net spread for her, and that must your daughter and her gentlewomen carry.° The sport will be when they hold one an opinion of another's dotage, and no such matter.[2] That's the scene that I would see, which will be merely° a dumb show.[3] Let us send her to call him in to dinner.

carry out

completely

[**Don Pedro**, **Leonato**, *and* **Claudio** *exit.*]

Benedick

[*coming forward*] This can be no trick. The conference° was sadly° borne; they have the truth of this from Hero; they seem to pity the lady. It seems her affections have their full bent.[4] Love me? Why, it must be requited!° I hear how I am censured. They say I will bear myself proudly if I perceive the love come from her. They say, too, that she will rather die than give any sign of affection. I did never think to marry. I must not seem proud. Happy are they that hear their detractions and can put them to mending.[5] They say the lady is fair; 'tis a truth, I can bear them witness. And virtuous; 'tis so, I cannot reprove° it. And wise, but° for loving me. By my troth, it is no addition to her wit—nor no great argument of

conversation

seriously

returned

refute / except

1 *it is no addition to her wit—nor no great argument of her folly*

It is no compliment to her intelligence, but neither is it evidence of her foolishness.

2 *I may chance have some odd quirks and remnants of wit broken on me*

I may perhaps have a few mocking quips and well-worn insults hurled at me.

3 *paper bullets*

Ineffective attacks

4 Enter **Beatrice**.

The ensuing dialogue provides a humorous break between the two eavesdropping scenes—the first broadly comic, the second shorter and more serious. In the 1993 Branagh film, Emma Thompson marches angrily to the orchard alley to find Kenneth Branagh's Benedick, who "has thrown what he thinks to be a gallant and sexy leg up on the edge of the fountain. He strikes a pose and a tone of voice that reminds one of Tony Curtis as Cary Grant in *Some Like It Hot*. It is a face frozen in a grin that is trying to convey sex, romance, intelligence, wit, and warmth, all at once. In short, he looks ridiculous" (see Branagh in For Further Reading).

i.e., exceedingly / *quips* / *ranted* / *i.e., food* / *odd sayings* / *intimidate / pursuit* / *inclination*

her folly,[1] for I will be horribly° in love with her! I may chance have some odd quirks° and remnants of wit broken on me[2] because I have railed° so long against marriage, but doth not the appetite alter? A man loves the meat° in his youth that he cannot endure in his age. Shall quips and sentences° and these paper bullets[3] of the brain awe° a man from the career° of his humor?° No! The world must be peopled! When I said I would die a bachelor, I did not think I should live till I were married. Here comes Beatrice. By this day, she's a fair lady. I do spy some marks of love in her.

Enter **Beatrice**.[4]

Beatrice

Against my will, I am sent to bid you come in to dinner.

Benedick

Fair Beatrice, I thank you for your pains.

Beatrice

I took no more pains for those thanks than you take pains to thank me. If it had been painful, I would not have come.

Benedick

You take pleasure then in the message?

Beatrice

small crow / with / *appetite*

Yea, just so much as you may take upon a knife's point and choke a daw° withal.° You have no stomach,° signior. Fare you well. *She exits.*

Benedick

Ha! "Against my will I am sent to bid you come in to dinner." There's a double meaning in that. "I took no

1 *Jew*

I.e., "ungenerous," a common slur derived from the fact that Jews were said to lack "Christian" charity. Many modern productions change this to "fool" or some other inoffensive insult.

2 *I will go get her picture.*

I.e., I will have a picture painted of her. Aristocratic lovers often had a miniature portrait of their beloved painted to be worn in a locket.

more pains for those thanks than you took pains to thank me." That's as much as to say, "Any pains that I take for you is as easy as thanks." If I do not take pity of° her, I am a villain. If I do not love her, I am a Jew.[1] I will go get her picture.[2] *He exits.*

on

1 *Ursley*

An affectionate diminutive of Ursula.

2 *pleachèd*

Overarched by intertwining branches; see 1.2.8 and note.

3 *like favorites / Made proud by princes, that advance their pride / Against that power that bred it*

Like favored coutiers, made arrogant by their rulers' affection, who dare to turn against those who had advanced them.

4 *Bear thee well in it*

Do it skillfully.

5 *only wounds by hearsay*

Wounds with mere gossip

Act 3, Scene 1

Enter **Hero** *and two gentlewomen,* **Margaret** *and* **Ursula**.

Hero

Good Margaret, run thee to the parlor.
There shalt thou find my cousin Beatrice
Talking Proposing° with the Prince and Claudio.
Whisper her ear and tell her I and Ursley[1]
conversation Walk in the orchard, and our whole discourse°
Is all of her. Say that thou overheard'st us,
And bid her steal into the pleachèd[2] bower
Where honeysuckles, ripened by the sun,
Forbid the sun to enter, like favorites
Made proud by princes, that advance their pride
Against that power that bred it.[3] There will she
herself hide her°
conversation / duty To listen our propose.° This is thy office.°
Bear thee well in it[4] and leave us alone.

Margaret

promise / immediately I'll make her come, I warrant° you, presently.°

[*She exits.*]

Hero

Now, Ursula, when Beatrice doth come,
walk / path As we do trace° this alley° up and down,
Our talk must only be of Benedick.
When I do name him, let it be thy part
To praise him more than ever man did merit.
My talk to thee must be how Benedick
material Is sick in love with Beatrice. Of this matter°
Is little Cupid's crafty arrow made,
That only wounds by hearsay.[5]

1 *lapwing*

Small bird that scurries on the ground, known for its skill in leading predators from its nest

2 *woodbine coverture*

Cover provided by the honeysuckle

Enter **Beatrice**, [*hiding*].

Now begin,
For look where Beatrice like a lapwing[1] runs
Close by the ground, to hear our conference.

Ursula

[*aside to* **Hero**] The pleasant'st angling is to see the fish
i.e., fins Cut with her golden oars° the silver stream
And greedily devour the treacherous bait.
So angle we for Beatrice, who even now
hidden Is couchèd° in the woodbine coverture.[2]
Fear you not my part of the dialogue.

Hero

[*aside to* **Ursula**] Then go we near her, that her ear lose nothing
Of the false sweet bait that we lay for it.
[*approaching* **Beatrice**] No, truly, Ursula, she is too disdainful.
unapproachable I know her spirits are as coy° and wild
wild female hawks / cliff As haggards° of the rock.°

Ursula

But are you sure
That Benedick loves Beatrice so entirely?

Hero

newly betrothed So says the Prince and my new-trothèd° lord.

Ursula

And did they bid you tell her of it, madam?

Hero

They did entreat me to acquaint her of it,
But I persuaded them, if they loved Benedick,

1 *All matter else seems weak*

Everyone else's conversation seems of little value.

2 *Nor take no shape nor project of affection*

Nor (can she) even imagine the form or function of love

3 *spell him backward*

Denigrate his best qualities; misrepresent him

4 *If black, why, nature, drawing of an antic, / Made a foul blot*

If he is swarthy, why, (she will say that) nature, while trying to draw a grotesque figure, produced an inky blotch.

5 *lance ill-headed*

Spear with a dull point

6 *agate very vilely cut*

Agates (semiprecious gems) were often carved with small figures; here her gibe is that he is not only small but also misshapen.

To wish him wrestle with affection
And never to let Beatrice know of it.

Ursula

Why did you so? Doth not the gentleman
fully Deserve as full° as fortunate a bed
lie down As ever Beatrice shall couch° upon?

Hero

O god of love! I know he doth deserve
credited As much as may be yielded° to a man,
But nature never framed a woman's heart
Of prouder stuff than that of Beatrice.
Disdain and scorn ride sparkling in her eyes,
Undervaluing Misprizing° what they look on, and her wit
Values itself so highly that to her
All matter else seems weak.[1] She cannot love,
Nor take no shape nor project of affection,[2]
in love with herself She is so self-endearèd.°

Ursula

Sure, I think so,
And therefore certainly it were not good
She knew his love, lest she'll make sport at it.

Hero

Why, you speak truth. I never yet saw man,
However / exceptionally How° wise, how noble, young, how rarely° featured,
But she would spell him backward.[3] If fair-faced,
She would swear the gentleman should be her sister;
olive-complexioned If black,° why, nature, drawing of an antic,
Made a foul blot;[4] if tall, a lance ill-headed;[5]
short If low,° an agate very vilely cut;[6]
weathervane If speaking, why, a vane° blown with all winds;
by If silent, why, a block movèd with° none.
So turns she every man the wrong side out

1 *from all fashions*

Contrary to normal behavior

2 *Out of myself*

I.e., into silence

3 *press me to death*

Alluding to the practice of torturing a prisoner by placing heavy weights on his chest. Because this form of torture was often used to force a confession, Hero's image suggests that Beatrice would mock her whether she spoke or remained silent.

4 *sighs*

Sighs were thought to drain blood from the heart.

And never gives to truth and virtue that
honesty / deserve Which simpleness° and merit purchaseth.°

Ursula

fault finding Sure, sure, such carping° is not commendable.

Hero

No. Not to be so odd and from all fashions,[1]
As Beatrice is, cannot be commendable.
But who dare tell her so? If I should speak,
nothingness She would mock me into air.° Oh, she would laugh
me
Out of myself,[2] press me to death[3] with wit.
Therefore let Benedick, like covered fire,
Consume away in sighs,[4] waste inwardly.
It were a better death than die with mocks,
Which is as bad as die with tickling.

Ursula

Yet tell her of it. Hear what she will say.

Hero

No. Rather I will go to Benedick
And counsel him to fight against his passion,
inconsequential And truly I'll devise some honest° slanders
To stain my cousin with. One doth not know
How much an ill word may empoison liking.

Ursula

Oh, do not do your cousin such a wrong!
She cannot be so much without true judgment,
Having so swift and excellent a wit
judged As she is prized° to have, as to refuse
So rare a gentleman as Signior Benedick.

Hero

i.e., best He is the only° man of Italy,
Always excepted my dear Claudio.

1 *Speaking my fancy*

I.e., if I state my own preference

2 *attires*

Clothing, perhaps specifically head-dresses or tiaras (cf. *tire* in 3.4.12)

3 *limed*

I.e., snared; birdlime was a sticky substance used to trap small birds on tree branches.

4 *What fire is in mine ears?*

Because Hero and Ursula were discussing her, Beatrice's ears are proverbially burning.

5 *No glory lives behind the back of such.*

Such characteristics are not praised by others. This speech (lines 107–116) marks the first time Beatrice speaks verse in the play. The actress Ellen Terry played her celebrated Beatrice (1882–1893) as "pleasant-spirited": "her eyes are clear and full of fire; her mouth is fine—intellectual with something of irony, of benevolence, and of reserve. A singular countenance where the mind and heart both rule." She found this moment of humbling self-revelation and strong emotion a great challenge: "Very difficult words for an actress; not very effective, but charged with the passion of a strong, deep heart! I have played Beatrice hundreds of times and never done this speech as I feel it should be done" (*Four Lectures on Shakespeare*, New York: Benjamin Blom, 1932, rpt. 1969, pp. 83, 88).

6 *Taming my wild heart*

Picking up the imagery of lines 35–36

Ursula

I pray you, be not angry with me, madam,
Speaking my fancy.[1] Signior Benedick,
reason For shape, for bearing, argument° and valor,
Goes foremost in report through Italy.

Hero

reputation Indeed, he hath an excellent good name.°

Ursula

His excellence did earn it, ere he had it.
When are you married, madam?

Hero

i.e., as of tomorrow Why, every day, tomorrow.° Come; go in.
I'll show thee some attires,[2] and have thy counsel
adorn Which is the best to furnish° me tomorrow.

[*They move aside.*]

Ursula

promise [*aside to* **Hero**] She's limed,[3] I warrant° you. We have caught her, madam.

Hero

[*aside to* **Ursula**] If it proves so, then loving goes by
chance haps;°
Some Cupid kills with arrows, some with traps.

[**Hero** *and* **Ursula** *exit.*]

Beatrice

[*coming forward*] What fire is in mine ears?[4] Can this be true?
Stand I condemned for pride and scorn so much?
Contempt, farewell, and maiden pride, adieu!
No glory lives behind the back of such.[5]
And Benedick, love on; I will requite thee,
Taming my wild heart[6] to thy loving hand.

1 *better than reportingly*

As more than hearsay

If thou dost love, my kindness shall incite thee
To bind our loves up in a holy band.° *bond; wedding band*
For others say thou dost deserve, and I
Believe it better than reportingly.[1] *She exits.*

1 *only be bold with Benedick*

Ask only Benedick

2 *cut Cupid's bow-string*

I.e., evaded falling in love

3 *Hang him, truant!*

I.e., it would serve him right; hang the cynic for his disdain.

4 *Draw it.*

Pull it (the tooth) out.

Act 3, Scene 2

Enter [**Don Pedro**], **Claudio**, **Benedick**, *and* **Leonato**.

Don Pedro

celebrated — I do but stay till your marriage be consummate,° and then go I toward Aragon.

Claudio

accompany / permit — I'll bring° you thither, my lord, if you'll vouchsafe° me.

Don Pedro

stain / *executioner (i.e., Cupid)* — Nay, that would be as great a soil° in the new gloss of your marriage as to show a child his new coat and forbid him to wear it. I will only be bold with Benedick[1] for his company, for, from the crown of his head to the sole of his foot, he is all mirth. He hath twice or thrice cut Cupid's bow-string,[2] and the little hangman° dare not shoot at him. He hath a heart as sound as a bell, and his tongue is the clapper, for what his heart thinks, his tongue speaks.

Benedick

Gentlemen — Gallants,° I am not as I have been.

Leonato

more serious — So say I. Methinks you are sadder.°

Claudio

I hope he be in love.

Don Pedro

sincere / *lacks* — Hang him, truant![3] There's no true° drop of blood in him to be truly touched with love. If he be sad, he wants° money.

Benedick

I have the toothache.

Don Pedro

Draw it.[4]

1 *Hang it!*

A common expression of frustration, but also here punning on the practice of hanging teeth outside a barber shop to advertise the availability of tooth extractions.

2 *You must hang it first and draw it afterwards.*

Claudio puns further, now on the practice of hanging and subsequently drawing (disemboweling) criminals.

3 *humor or a worm*

Toothaches were thought to be caused by toxic bodily fluids (*humors*) or infestations of worms inside the teeth.

4 *strange disguises*

The influence of European fashions on Elizabethan dress was often an object of satire on the London stage.

5 *a Spaniard from the hip upward, no doublet*

I.e., wearing a Spanish cape rather than an English jacket.

6 *the old ornament of his cheek hath already stuffed tennis balls*

His beard has already been cut and sent to stuff tennis balls (common practice at the time). Beatrice does not like beards; see 2.1.25–26.

Benedick

Hang it![1]

Claudio

You must hang it first and draw it afterwards.[2]

Don Pedro

What, sigh for the toothache?

Leonato

Where there Where° is but a humor or a worm.[3]

Benedick

except Well, everyone can master a grief but° he that has it.

Claudio

Yet say I, he is in love.

Don Pedro

love There is no appearance of fancy° in him, unless it be
attraction a fancy° that he hath to strange disguises,[4] as to be a
Dutchman today, a Frenchman tomorrow, or in the
shape of two countries at once, as a German from the
baggy trousers waist downward, all slops,° and a Spaniard from the
hip upward, no doublet.[5] Unless he have a fancy to
this foolery, as it appears he hath, he is no fool for
love fancy,° as you would have it appear he is.

Claudio

If he be not in love with some woman, there is no
He believing old signs. 'A° brushes his hat o' mornings.
What should that bode?

Don Pedro

Hath any man seen him at the barber's?

Claudio

No, but the barber's man hath been seen with him,
and the old ornament of his cheek hath already
stuffed tennis balls.[6]

1 *smell him out*

Learn his secret (but punning on the literal sense: "smell his presence")

2 *wash his face*

Probably, bathe his face in perfume rather than with soap and water.

3 *paint himself*

Use cosmetics

4 *what they say of him*

The gossip about him

5 *governed by stops*

Ruled by restraint. *Stops* literally refers to the frets on a lute, an instrument commonly identified with love songs.

6 *dies for him*

Pines for him, though, in Elizabethan slang, *die* also meant "reach orgasm," a sense which Don Pedro's following line jokes upon.

Leonato

Indeed, he looks younger than he did by the loss of a beard.

Don Pedro

perfume Nay, 'a rubs himself with civet.° Can you smell him out[1] by that?

Claudio

That's as much as to say the sweet youth's in love.

Don Pedro

evidence The greatest note° of it is his melancholy.

Claudio

And when was he wont to wash his face?[2]

Don Pedro

i.e., his use of cosmetics Yea, or to paint himself?[3] For the which,° I hear what they say of him.[4]

Claudio

but what of Nay, but° his jesting spirit, which is now crept into a lute string and now governed by stops?[5]

Don Pedro

sad Indeed, that tells a heavy° tale for him. Conclude; conclude: he is in love.

Claudio

Nay, but I know who loves him.

Don Pedro

guarantee That would I know too. I warrant,° one that knows him not.

Claudio

qualities Yes, and his ill conditions,° and, in despite of all, dies for him.[6]

Don Pedro

She shall be buried with her face upwards.

1 *to break*

He goes to speak

2 *Hero and Margaret*

In 3.1.15ff., it is Hero and Ursula who trick Beatrice; either Shakespeare has forgotten, or Claudio makes a mistake, assuming Margaret is the more likely person to play this role.

3 *If your leisure served*

If you have the time; if it's convenient for you

Benedick

Yet is this no charm for the toothache.—Old signior, walk aside with me. I have studied eight or nine wise words to speak to you, which these hobbyhorses° must not hear. [**Benedick** *and* **Leonato** *exit.*]

buffoons

Don Pedro

For° my life, to break[1] with him about Beatrice!

Upon

Claudio

'Tis even so. Hero and Margaret[2] have by this° played their parts with Beatrice, and then the two bears will not bite one another when they meet.

now

Enter [**Don**] **John**, *the bastard.*

Don John

My lord and brother, God save you.

Don Pedro

Good e'en,° brother.

i.e., evening

Don John

If your leisure served,[3] I would speak with you.

Don Pedro

In private?

Don John

If it please you. Yet Count Claudio may hear, for what I would speak of concerns him.

Don Pedro

What's the matter?

Don John

[*to* **Claudio**] Means your Lordship to be married tomorrow?

Don Pedro

You know he does.

1 *aim better at*

Think more highly of

2 *dearness of heart*

Friendship

3 *circumstances shortened*

In brief; ignoring the details

4 *too long a-talking of*

Been too long the subject of our conversation

5 *paint out*

Depict; convey

Don John

I know not that, when he knows what I know.

Claudio

If there be any impediment, I pray you discover° it.

reveal

Don John

You may think I love you not. Let that appear hereafter, and aim better at[1] me by° that I now will manifest. For° my brother, I think he holds you well,° and in dearness of heart[2] hath holp° to effect your ensuing marriage—surely suit° ill spent and labor ill bestowed.

for / *As for / in high regard* / *helped* / *courtship*

Don Pedro

Why, what's the matter?

Don John

I came hither to tell you; and, circumstances shortened,[3] for she has been too long a-talking of,[4] the lady is disloyal.°

unfaithful

Claudio

Who? Hero?

Don John

Even she: Leonato's Hero, your Hero, every man's Hero.

Claudio

Disloyal?

Don John

The word is too good to paint out[5] her wickedness. I could say she were worse. Think you of a worse title, and I will fit her to it. Wonder not till further warrant.° Go° but with me tonight, you shall see her chamber window entered, even the night before her wedding day. If you love her then, tomorrow wed her, but it would better fit your honor° to change your mind.

proof / *i.e., If you go* / *reputation*

Claudio

[to **Don Pedro**] May this be so?

1 *If you dare not trust that you see, confess not that you know.*

If you are not willing to see for yourself, then do not profess to know.

2 *untowardly turned*

Unhappily transformed

3 *mischief strangely thwarting*

Wickedness (i.e., Hero's infidelity) unaccountably destructive

4 *the sequel*

I.e., what will then happen. Don John promises that spectators shall see Hero's *chamber window entered* (3.2.98–99) but they apparently see no such thing: Borachio says that Margaret leans out of Hero's chamber window and talks with him (3.3.133–138), and that is exactly what Claudio and Don Pedro charge at the wedding (4.1.81–82, 87–89). Borachio also says later in his confession that he courted Margaret *in Hero's garments* (5.1.230–231). Many directors have added some representation of Borachio's encounter with Margaret (see Cox in For Further Reading). Branagh's 1993 film showed Borachio and Margaret making love in silhouette on a balcony; it then cut to the shaking trio of onlookers, Claudio, Don Pedro, and Don John and ended with a close-up of Robert Sean Leonard's Claudio, weeping in shock and anger. But Shakespeare chose not to stage this scene and thus to leave Claudio's character more open to the charges of gullibility, rashness, and jealousy.

Don Pedro

I will not think it.

Don John

If you dare not trust that you see, confess not that you know.[1] If you will follow me, I will show you enough, and, when you have seen more and heard more, proceed accordingly.

Claudio

If I see anything tonight why I should not marry her, tomorrow in the congregation, where I should wed, there will I shame her.

Don Pedro

since; just as And as° I wooed for thee to obtain her, I will join with thee to disgrace her.

Don John

I will disparage her no farther till you are my witnesses. *calmly / outcome* Bear it coldly° but till midnight and let the issue° show itself.

Don Pedro

O day untowardly turned![2]

Claudio

O mischief strangely thwarting![3]

Don John

calamity O plague° right well prevented! So will you say when you have seen the sequel.[4] [*They exit.*]

1 the watch

A group of citizens whose duties as civic watchmen included announcing the hour and simple acts of policing

2 *but they*

If they did not

3 *salvation*

For "damnation." Both Dogberry and Verges frequently misspeak to comic effect, saying the opposite of what they intend.

4 *constable*

Deputy commander of the watch; Dogberry himself is the *Master Constable* (line 15).

5 *George Seacole*

Usually identified as the name of the Second Watchman since he seems to be the one who responds to Dogberry's summons in line 12 (though the speech prefix in the Quarto is merely *Watch 2*). Throughout the scene, speech prefixes for the individual watchmen are imprecise, allowing for various assignments of lines. Shakespeare seems to be careless about the specific speech assignments here, but is obviously fond of this comically incongruous English name in Messina, as Dogberry calls the sexton (town clerk) *Francis Seacole* (3.5.50).

6 *a good name*

Coal shipped from Newcastle ("sea coal") was considered to be of exceptional quality.

Act 3, Scene 3

Enter **Dogberry** *and his compartner* [**Verges**,] *with the watch.*[1]

Dogberry

Are you good men and true?

Verges

Yea, or else it were pity but they[2] should suffer salvation,[3] body and soul.

Dogberry

Nay, that were a punishment too good for them, if they should have any allegiance° in them, being chosen for the Prince's watch.

(error for "disloyalty")

Verges

Well, give them their charge,° neighbor Dogberry.

assignment

Dogberry

First, who think you the most desartless° man to be constable?[4]

(error for "deserving")

First Watchman

Hugh Otecake, sir, or George Seacole,[5] for they can write and read.

Dogberry

Come hither, neighbor Seacole. God hath blessed you with a good name.[6] To be a well-favored° man is the gift of fortune, but to write and read comes by nature.

handsome

Seacole

Both which, Master Constable—

Dogberry

You have. I knew it would be your answer. Well, for your favor,° sir, why, give God thanks and make no boast of it, and for your writing and reading, let that appear when there is no need of such vanity.° You are thought here to be the most senseless° and fit man for the constable of the watch; therefore bear you the lantern.

looks

foolishness

(error for "sensible")

1 *vagrom*

Mispronunciation of "vagrant"

2 *belongs to*

Are the responsibilities of

3 *bills*

Long-handled weapons, used by watchmen, with both a spearhead and an axe-like blade

(error for "apprehend") This is your charge: you shall comprehend° all
halt vagrom[1] men; you are to bid any man stand° in the Prince's name.

Seacole

he How if 'a° will not stand?

Dogberry

Why, then, take no note of him, but let him go and
immediately presently° call the rest of the watch together and thank God you are rid of a knave.

Verges

If he will not stand when he is bidden, he is none of the Prince's subjects.

Dogberry

True, and they are to meddle with none but the Prince's subjects.—You shall also make no noise in the streets, for, for the watch to babble and to talk is
(error for "intolerable") most tolerable° and not to be endured.

First Watchman

We will rather sleep than talk. We know what belongs to[2] a watch.

Dogberry

experienced Why, you speak like an ancient° and most quiet watchman, for I cannot see how sleeping should offend. Only have a care that your bills[3] be not stolen. Well, you are to call at all the alehouses and bid those that are drunk get them to bed.

First Watchman

How if they will not?

Dogberry

Why, then let them alone till they are sober. If they
more accomodating make you not then the better° answer, you may say they are not the men you took them for.

1 *more is*

The better it is

2 *they that touch pitch will be defiled*

This maxim is paraphrased from the Apocryphal book of Ecclesiasticus (13:1). *Pitch* is a sticky tar-like substance.

3 *by my will*

Willingly

First Watchman

Well, sir.

Dogberry

honest / *have to do*

If you meet a thief, you may suspect him, by virtue of your office, to be no true° man, and for such kind of men, the less you meddle or make° with them, why the more is[1] for your honesty.

Seacole

If we know him to be a thief, shall we not lay hands on him?

Dogberry

apprehend

Truly, by your office you may, but I think they that touch pitch will be defiled.[2] The most peaceable way for you, if you do take° a thief, is to let him show himself what he is and steal out of your company.

Verges

You have been always called a merciful man, partner.

Dogberry

(error for "less")

Truly, I would not hang a dog by my will,[3] much more° a man who hath any honesty in him.

Verges

calm

[*to the watch*] If you hear a child cry in the night, you must call to the nurse and bid her still° it.

Seacole

How if the nurse be asleep and will not hear us?

Dogberry

Why, then depart in peace and let the child wake her with crying, for the ewe that will not hear her lamb when it baas will never answer a calf when he bleats.

Verges

'Tis very true.

1 *by 'r lady*

A mild oath, "by our lady"

Dogberry

This is the end of the charge. You, constable, are to
i.e., represent present° the Prince's own person. If you meet the
stop Prince in the night, you may stay° him.

Verges

he Nay, by 'r lady,[1] that I think 'a° cannot.

Dogberry

Five shillings to one on 't, with any man that knows
unless the statutes, he may stay him—marry, not without°
the Prince be willing, for indeed the watch ought
to offend no man, and it is an offense to stay a man
against his will.

Verges

By 'r lady, I think it be so.

Dogberry

If Ha! Ah ha!—Well, masters, good night. An° there be
that occurs any matter of weight chances,° call up me. Keep your
fellows' counsels and your own, and good night.
—Come, neighbor.

Seacole

Well, masters, we hear our charge. Let us go sit here upon the church bench till two, and then all to bed.

Dogberry

One word more, honest neighbors. I pray you watch
about Signior Leonato's door, for the wedding being
bustle; commotion there tomorrow, there is a great coil° tonight. Adieu.
(error for "vigilant") Be vigitant,° I beseech you.

[**Dogberry** *and* **Verges**] *exit.*

Enter **Borachio** *and* **Conrade**.

Borachio

What, Conrade!

1 *Mass*

An oath, "by the mass"

2 *my elbow itched*

Itching elbows proverbially foretold bad company.

3 *scab*

Literally, a skin lesion; figuratively, a scoundrel

4 *like a true drunkard*

It is a commonplace that drunkards will tell everything they know; see also p. 80, note 6.

5 *yet stand close*

Stay hidden for now.

6 *is nothing to*

Does not say anything about

Seacole

[*to the watch*] Peace! Stir not.

Borachio

Conrade, I say!

Conrade

Here, man; I am at thy elbow.

Borachio

Mass,[1] and my elbow itched.[2] I thought there would a scab[3] follow.

Conrade

I will owe thee an answer for that. And now forward with thy tale.

Borachio

sloped roof Stand thee close, then, under this penthouse,° for it drizzles rain, and I will, like a true drunkard,[4] utter all to thee.

Seacole

[*to the watch*] Some treason, masters; yet stand close.[5]

Borachio

Therefore know I have earned of Don John a thousand ducats.

Conrade

expensive Is it possible that any villainy should be so dear?°

Borachio

Thou shouldst rather ask if it were possible any villainy should be so rich, for when rich villains have need of *charge* poor ones, poor ones may make° what price they will.

Conrade

I wonder at it.

Borachio

inexperienced That shows thou art unconfirmed.° Thou knowest *jacket* that the fashion of a doublet,° or a hat, or a cloak, is nothing to[6] a man.

1 *it is apparel*

Conrade takes *is nothing to* as "means nothing to."

2 *I know that Deformed.*

The watchman takes Borachio's metaphorical description of fashion as a *deformed thief* to mean that a member of the criminal party is named *Deformed*.

3 *goes up and down*

Walks around

4 *Pharaoh's soldiers in the reechy painting*

Most likely refers to a picture of the Egyptian soldiers drowning in the Red Sea (Exodus 14:13–28); *reechy* means dirty; smoke discolored.

5 *Bel's priests*

Baal (*Bel*), a Babylonian god, and his seventy priests are the subject of a story in the Apocrypha.

6 *shaven Hercules*

Possibly referring to a popular emblematic representation of the youthful Hercules at the crossroads of virtue and vice

7 *codpiece*

A pouch, often conspicuous and ornate, worn over the crotch of a man's breeches

8 *the fashion wears out more apparel than the man*

Changing fashion uses up more clothing than the wearer does.

Conrade

Yes, it is apparel.[1]

Borachio

I mean the fashion.

Conrade

Yes, the fashion is the fashion.

Borachio

(an exclamation) *deforming*

Tush,° I may as well say the fool's the fool. But see'st thou not what a deformed° thief this fashion is?

Seacole

He

[*to the watch*] I know that Deformed.[2] 'A° has been a vile thief this seven year. 'A goes up and down[3] like a gentleman. I remember his name.

Borachio

Didst thou not hear somebody?

Conrade

weathervane

No; 'twas the vane° on the house.

Borachio

fashionable gentlemen *massive*

See'st thou not, I say, what a deformed thief this fashion is, how giddily 'a turns about all the hot-bloods° between fourteen and five-and-thirty, sometimes fashioning them like Pharaoh's soldiers in the reechy painting,[4] sometime like god Bel's priests[5] in the old church-window, sometime like the shaven Hercules[6] in the smirched worm-eaten tapestry, where his codpiece[7] seems as massy° as his club?

Conrade

All this I see, and I see that the fashion wears out more apparel than the man.[8] But art not thou thyself giddy with the fashion too, that thou hast shifted out of thy tale into telling me of the fashion?

1 *by the name of Hero*

While calling her "Hero"

2 *leans me out*

Leans out toward me

3 *as he was appointed*

As he had arranged to do

4 *recovered the most dangerous piece of lechery*

I.e., discovered the most dangerous case of treachery

5 *lock*

A "lovelock," a long strand of hair, often ornamented, a common affectation of young gentlemen

Borachio

Not so, neither. But know that I have tonight wooed
Margaret, the lady Hero's gentlewoman, by the name
of Hero.[1] She leans me out[2] at her mistress' chamber
window, bids me a thousand times good night. I tell
poorly this tale vilely.° I should first tell thee how the Prince,
Claudio, and my master, planted and placed and pos-
instructed sessed° by my master Don John, saw afar off in the
amorous orchard this amiable° encounter.

Conrade

And thought they Margaret was Hero?

Borachio

Two of them did, the Prince and Claudio, but the devil
my master knew she was Margaret—and partly by
influenced his oaths, which first possessed° them, partly by the
dark night, which did deceive them, but chiefly by
my villainy, which did confirm any slander that Don
John had made, away went Claudio enraged, swore he
would meet her as he was appointed[3] next morning
church at the temple,° and there, before the whole congregation, shame her with what he saw o'ernight and send
her home again without a husband.

First Watchman

[*coming forward*] We charge you, in the Prince's name,
halt stand!°

Seacole

i.e., upstanding Call up the right° Master Constable. We have here
recovered the most dangerous piece of lechery[4]
that ever was known in the commonwealth.

First Watchman

he And one Deformed is one of them. I know him; 'a°
wears a lock.[5] [*He exits.*]

1 *Masters— / Never speak, we charge you; let us obey you to go with us.*

The Quarto assigns these lines to Conrade, but, unlike the watch, he does not speak in comic malapropism and, as a prisoner, has no business giving orders. To resolve the problem, some have had Dogberry enter at line 153 (cf. *Call up the right Master Constable*, 152) and reassigned line 155 and these lines to him. As Lewis Theobald conjectured in the early 18th century, however, the textual confusions can more simply and plausibly be resolved by the insertion of a speech prefix after *Masters* (3.3.160), which reassigns the remaining lines to a watchman. See Stanley Wells, "A Crux in *Much Ado About Nothing*, III.iii.152–163," *Shakespeare Quarterly*, 31 (1980) 85–86.

2 *goodly commodity*

Valuable item

3 *being taken up of these men's bills*

Punning on several senses of *taken up* and *bills*: (1) being arrested at the point of these watchmen's weapons; (2) being incarcerated on the authority of their warrants; (3) being purchased with their credit

4 *in question*

(1) subject to prosecution; (2) of doubtful value

Conrade

Masters, masters—

Seacole

[*to* **Borachio**] You'll be made bring Deformed forth, I warrant you.

Conrade

Masters—

Seacole

(error for "order") Never speak, we charge you; let us obey° you to go with us.[1]

Borachio

[*to* **Conrade**] We are like to prove a goodly commodity,[2] being taken up of these men's bills.[3]

Conrade

A commodity in question,[4] I warrant you.—Come, we'll obey you. *They exit.*

1 *rebato*

A stiff ornamented collar

Act 3, Scene 4

Enter **Hero** *and* **Margaret**, *and* **Ursula**.

Hero

Good Ursula, wake my cousin Beatrice and desire her to rise.

Ursula

I will, lady.

Hero

And bid her come hither.

Ursula

Very well Well.° [*She exits.*]

Margaret

In faith Troth,° I think your other rebato[1] were better.

Hero

No, pray thee, good Meg, I'll wear this.

Margaret

it's / guarantee By my troth, 's° not so good, and I warrant° your cousin will say so.

Hero

My cousin's a fool, and thou art another. I'll wear none but this.

Margaret

ornamented hairpiece *bit / excellent* I like the new tire° within excellently, if the hair were a thought° browner; and your gown's a most rare° fashion, i' faith. I saw the Duchess of Milan's gown that they praise so.

Hero

is exceptional Oh, that exceeds,° they say.

1 *in respect of*

Compared with

2 *cloth o' gold, and cuts, and laced with silver, set with pearls, down sleeves, side sleeves, and skirts round underborne with a bluish tinsel*

Fabric woven partly with gold thread, and slits (*cuts*, to reveal the fabric underneath), ornamented with silver lace, beaded with pearls, with tight sleeves to the wrist (*down sleeves*) and ornamented sleeves hanging from the shoulders (*side sleeves*), with the lower portion (*skirts*) trimmed at the bottom (*underborne*) with shimmering fabric

3 *Saving your reverence*

I.e., pardon the expression

Margaret

By my troth, 's° but a nightgown° in respect of[1] yours—cloth o' gold, and cuts,° and laced with silver, set with pearls, down sleeves, side sleeves, and skirts round underborne with a bluish tinsel.[2] But for a fine, quaint,° graceful, and excellent fashion, yours is worth ten on° 't.

it's / dressing gown · *slits* · *ingeniously made* · *of*

Hero

God give me joy to wear it, for my heart is exceeding heavy.

Margaret

'Twill be heavier soon by the weight of a man.

Hero

Fie upon thee! Art not ashamed?

Margaret

Of what, lady? Of speaking honorably? Is not marriage honorable in° a beggar? Is not your lord honorable without marriage? I think you would have me say, "Saving your reverence,[3] a husband." An° bad thinking do not wrest° true speaking, I'll offend nobody. Is there any harm in "the heavier for a husband"? None, I think, an° it be the right husband and the right wife. Otherwise, 'tis light° and not heavy. Ask my Lady Beatrice else. Here she comes.

even in · *If* · *pervert* · *if* · *wanton*

Enter **Beatrice**.

Hero

Good morrow, coz.°

cousin; kinswoman

Beatrice

Good morrow, sweet Hero.

Hero

Why, how now? Do you speak in the sick tune?

1 *Clap 's into "Light o' love." That goes without a burden.*

Margaret asks Beatrice to clap her hands in rhythm so that the women can begin singing the popular song "Light o' love," which has no *burden*, or bass part. With its connotations of masculine weight, *burden* continues Margaret's mischievous jokes about women bearing the weight of a man during sexual intercourse.

2 *Ye light o' love, with your heels!*

You make light of love with your (1) dancing; (2) promiscuity. "Light heeled" was a colloquialism meaning "promiscuous," and Margaret has already punned on *light* meaning "wanton" at line 34.

3 *barns*

A pun on *bairns*, meaning "children"

4 *O illegitimate construction!*

Both "What a forced joke!" (*illegitimate construction* implying a faulty or strained interpretation) and "Oh, bastard children!" (continuing the earlier pun on *bairns/barns*)

5 *scorn that with my heels*

Reject that by kicking it away (a proverbial expression)

6 *Heigh-ho! / For a hawk, a horse, or a husband?*

Beatrice sighs *Heigh-ho!* as an expression of her melancholy, but, as the term is also used in hunting (to encourage hawks and horses), Margaret teasingly asks Beatrice whom she calls for. "Heigh-ho for a husband" was the title of a popular ballad, referred to by Beatrice at 2.1.287.

7 *For the letter that begins them all: H.*

***H* and *ache* were both pronounced "aitch" in Elizabethan English.**

8 *an you be not turned Turk*

I.e., if you have not abandoned your conviction (to scorn love). To "turn Turk" was a colloquial expression meaning "to abandon one's faith."

9 *no more sailing by the star*

I.e., nothing can be trusted anymore (literally, "the North Star can no longer be used for navigation").

10 *I am stuffed*

"I have a stuffy nose." Margaret goes on to joke that Beatrice cannot be both *a maid* (virgin) and *stuffed* (in the sexual sense).

Beatrice

I am out of all other tune, methinks.

Margaret

us Clap 's° into "Light o' love." That goes without a burden.[1] Do you sing it, and I'll dance it.

Beatrice

Ye light o' love, with your heels![2] Then, if your husband have stables enough, you'll see he shall lack no barns.[3]

Margaret

O illegitimate construction![4] I scorn that with my heels.[5]

Beatrice

'Tis almost five o'clock, cousin. 'Tis time you were ready. By my troth, I am exceeding ill. Heigh-ho!

Margaret

For a hawk, a horse, or a husband?[6]

Beatrice

For the letter that begins them all: H.[7]

Margaret

Well, an you be not turned Turk,[8] there's no more sailing by the star.[9]

Beatrice

I wonder What means the fool, trow?°

Margaret

Nothing, I; but God send everyone their heart's desire.

Hero

have These gloves the Count sent me, they are° an excellent perfume.

Beatrice

I am stuffed,[10] cousin. I cannot smell.

Margaret

A maid and stuffed? There's goodly catching of cold.

1 *professed apprehension*

I.e., thought yourself to be clever

2 *in your cap*

As though it were a coxcomb or a foolscap, the headgear traditionally worn by fools

3 carduus benedictus

I.e., the blessed thistle (see line 71), a well-known medicinal herb; punning on *cordis* (Latin for "in the heart") and *Benedick*

4 *There thou prick'st her with a thistle.*

I.e., that goes right to the heart of the matter (with a sexual joke on *prick'st*).

5 *Benedick was such another*

I.e., Benedick was another person who forswore love

6 *in despite of his heart, he eats his meat without grudging*

I.e., in spite of his previous refusal to love, he is now a man with normal appetites.

7 *Not a false gallop.*

I.e., I speak quickly but not untruly.

Beatrice

Oh, God help me; God help me! How long have you professed apprehension?[1]

Margaret

abandoned Even since you left° it. Doth not my wit become me
excellently rarely?°

Beatrice

It is not seen enough; you should wear it in your cap.[2]
faith By my troth,° I am sick.

Margaret

Get you some of this distilled *carduus benedictus*[3] and lay
fainting spell it to your heart. It is the only thing for a qualm.°

Hero

There thou prick'st her with a thistle.[4]

Beatrice

hidden meaning *Benedictus*? Why *benedictus*? You have some moral° in this *benedictus*?

Margaret

Moral? No, by my troth. I have no moral meaning. I meant
perhaps plain holy thistle. You may think perchance° that I think you are in love. Nay, by 'r lady, I am not such a fool to think
please what I list,° nor I list not to think what I can, nor indeed I cannot think, if I would think my heart out of thinking, that you are in love or that you will be in love or that you can be in love. Yet Benedick was such another,[5] and now is he become a man. He swore he would never marry, and
spite yet now, in despite° of his heart, he eats his meat without grudging.[6] And how you may be converted I know not, but methinks you look with your eyes as other women do.

Beatrice

What pace is this that thy tongue keeps?

Margaret

Not a false gallop.[7]

Enter **Ursula**.

Ursula

Madam, withdraw. The Prince, the Count, Signior Benedick, Don John, and all the gallants of the town are come to fetch you to church.

Hero

Help to dress me, good coz, good Meg, good Ursula.

[They exit.]

1 headborough

A minor officer of the watch; a petty constable

2 *Goodman*

Generic form of address to a commoner

3 *honest as the skin between his brows*

Proverbial, perhaps because of the idea that an honest man's forehead would not be furrowed by conscience, or because some felonies were punished by branding the forehead

4 Palabras

I.e., get to the point (from *pocas palabras*, Spanish for "few words").

5 *the poor Duke's*

For "the Duke's poor"

Act 3, Scene 5

Enter **Leonato** *and* [**Dogberry**] *the constable and* [**Verges**] *the headborough.*[1]

Leonato

What would you with me, honest neighbor?

Dogberry

(error for "conference") Marry, sir, I would have some confidence° with you
(error for "concerns") that discerns° you nearly.

Leonato

Briefly Brief,° I pray you, for you see it is a busy time with me.

Dogberry

Marry, this it is, sir.

Verges

Yes, in truth it is, sir.

Leonato

What is it, my good friends?

Dogberry

subject Goodman[2] Verges, sir, speaks a little off the matter.°
(error for "sharp") An old man, sir, and his wits are not so blunt° as, God help, I would desire they were, but, in faith, honest as the skin between his brows.[3]

Verges

Yes. I thank God I am as honest as any man living that is an old man and no honester than I.

Dogberry

(error for "odious") Comparisons are odorous.° *Palabras,*[4] neighbor Verges.

Leonato

Neighbors, you are tedious.

Dogberry

It pleases your Worship to say so, but we are the poor Duke's[5] officers. But truly, for mine own part, if I were

1 *tedious as a king*

Dogberry evidently thinks that *tedious* means "wealthy."

2 *exclamation on*

In Shakespeare's English, to *exclaim on* meant "to accuse"; Dogberry probably intends "acclamation on," or "praise for."

3 *excepting your Worship's presence*

Verges intends to say "respecting your Worship's presence," a phrase that was used to apologize in advance for saying something that might be found offensive.

4 *ha' ta'en*

Have taken

5 *"When the age is in, the wit is out."*

The proverb that Dogberry attempts to reproduce here properly goes, "When the ale is in, the wit is out." Dogberry subsequently offers several more proverbs, all ungarbled.

6 *he comes too short of you*

I.e., he cannot equal you (in wit or words), though perhaps the joke is also that the actor playing Dogberry was big and the one playing Verges was small and slender.

as tedious as a king,[1] I could find in my heart to
on bestow it all of° your Worship.

Leonato

All thy tediousness on me, ah?

Dogberry

if Yea, an° 'twere a thousand pound more than 'tis, for I hear as good exclamation on[2] your Worship as of any man in the city, and, though I be but a poor man, I am glad to hear it.

Verges

And so am I.

Leonato

gladly I would fain° know what you have to say.

Verges

last night Marry, sir, our watch tonight,° excepting your
absolute Worship's presence,[3] ha' ta'en[4] a couple of as arrant°
villains knaves° as any in Messina.

Dogberry

A good old man, sir. He will be talking. As they say, "When the age is in, the wit is out."[5] God help us, it is a world to see—Well said, i' faith, neighbor Verges.
If —Well, God's a good man. An° two men ride of a horse, one must ride behind. An honest soul, i' faith, sir, by my troth he is, as ever broke bread, but God is to be worshipped; all men are not alike, alas, good neighbor!

Leonato

Indeed, neighbor, he comes too short of you.[6]

Dogberry

Gifts that God gives.

Leonato

I must leave you.

Dogberry

(error for "apprehended") One word, sir. Our watch, sir, have indeed comprehended°

1 *Francis Seacole*

Presumably the name of the Sexton who appears in 4.2, but possibly a mistake for George Seacole of the watch, who *can write and read* (3.3.10).

2 *Here's that*

Here is that which (i.e., his brain, as Dogberry points to his head)

3 *noncome*

Error for *non plus* (bafflement); Dogberry may be thinking of *non compos mentis* ("not of sound mind").

(error for "suspicious") two auspicious° persons, and we would have them this morning examined before your Worship.

Leonato

testimony Take their examination° yourself and bring it me. I am now in great haste, as it may appear unto you.

Dogberry

(error for "sufficient") It shall be suffigance.°

Leonato

Drink some wine ere you go. Fare you well.

[*Enter a* **Messenger**.]

Messenger

wait My lord, they stay° for you to give your daughter to her husband.

Leonato

I'll wait upon them. I am ready.

He exits [*with* **Messenger**].

Dogberry

Go, good partner, go; get you to Francis Seacole.[1] Bid him bring his pen and inkhorn to the jail. We are now

(error for "examine") to examination° these men.

Verges

And we must do it wisely.

Dogberry

We will spare for no wit, I warrant you. Here's that[2] shall drive some of them to a noncome.[3] Only get the

(error for "examination") learned writer to set down our excommunication° and meet me at the jail. [*They exit.*]

1 *Friar Francis*

One of Shakespeare's several friars, Friar Francis, probably a Franciscan, sees through the deceit and suggests the temporizing strategy, the false report of Hero's death. (Compare the similar report of Helena's death in *All's Well That Ends Well.*) The friar uses the loaded image of burning heretics at the stake to express his conviction of Hero's innocence: *And in her eye there hath appeared a fire / To burn the errors that these Princes hold / Against her maiden truth* (4.1.160–162; cf. 1.1.202–203). This friar is a more sympathetic character than Friar Laurence of *Romeo and Juliet*, who is cowardly in Act Five, or the Duke disguised as a friar in *Measure for Measure*. Friar Francis will preside over the weddings and general reconciliation of 5.4.

2 *particular duties*

Responsibilities of each partner in the marriage (which Leonato, in his eagerness to get them married, does not want to be read)

Act 4, Scene 1

Enter [**Don Pedro**], [**Don John** *the*] *bastard*, **Leonato**, **Friar** [**Francis**], **Claudio**, **Benedick**, **Hero**, *and* **Beatrice**, [*with attendants*].

Leonato

service; ceremony Come, Friar Francis,[1] be brief: only to the plain form° of marriage, and you shall recount their particular duties[2] afterwards.

Friar Francis

[*to* **Claudio**] You come hither, my lord, to marry this lady?

Claudio

No.

Leonato

To be married to her.—Friar, you come to marry her.

Friar Francis

Lady, you come hither to be married to this count?

Hero

I do.

Friar Francis

undisclosed If either of you know any inward° impediment why you should not be conjoined, I charge you on your souls to utter it.

Claudio

Know you any, Hero?

Hero

None, my lord.

Friar Francis

Know you any, Count?

Leonato

I dare make his answer: none.

1 *interjections? Why, then, some be of laughing, as, "ah, ha, he!"*

Benedick quotes from the section on *interjections* in William Lyly's 1538 grammar book for school children.

2 *Father, by your leave*

Father, with your permission. Claudio's sarcasm goes undetected by Leonato, but anticipates the shaming of Hero.

3 *unconstrainèd soul*

Clear conscience

4 *unless you render her again*

Unless you were to take her and then return her in exchange (as nothing could equal Hero's value except Hero herself)

5 *Comes not that blood as modest evidence / To witness simple virtue?*

Doesn't that blush appear in her cheeks as evidence of her modesty, testifying to her innocence?

6 *What do you mean*

What are you talking about? Claudio then takes the question to be "what do you intend to do?"

Claudio

Oh, what men dare do! What men may do! What men daily do, not knowing what they do!

Benedick

How now, interjections? Why, then, some be of laughing, as, "ah, ha, he!"[1]

Claudio

aside / i.e. Leonato Stand thee by,° Friar.—Father,° by your leave,[2]
Will you with free and unconstrainèd soul[3]
Give me this maid, your daughter?

Leonato

As freely, son, as God did give her me.

Claudio

And what have I to give you back whose worth
equal May counterpoise° this rich and precious gift?

Don Pedro

Nothing, unless you render her again.[4]

Claudio

teach Sweet Prince, you learn° me noble thankfulness.
—There, Leonato, take her back again.
Give not this rotten orange to your friend.
mere show / appearance She's but the sign° and semblance° of her honor.
Behold how like a maid she blushes here!
Oh, what authority and show of truth
with Can cunning sin cover itself withal!°
blush Comes not that blood° as modest evidence
bear witness to To witness° simple virtue?[5] Would you not swear,
All you that see her, that she were a maid
By these exterior shows? But she is none.
lustful She knows the heat of a luxurious° bed.
Her blush is guiltiness, not modesty.

Leonato

What do you mean,[6] my lord?

1 *And so extenuate the forehand sin*

And thereby excuse the sin made before (but in expectation of) marriage

2 *Out on thee, seeming!*

(1) curse you, seeming virgin; (2) curse you, false appearances!

3 *write against it*

Publicly denounce it

4 *Dian in her orb*

Diana, the virgin goddess of the hunt, was associated with the moon. *In her orb* may either mean "in her orb-like (spherical) form" or "traveling in her orb," alluding to the Renaissance belief that the moon, stars, and planets revolved around the Earth embedded in individual, crystalline spheres.

5 *ere it be blown*

Before it blossoms

6 *Venus*

Roman goddess of love, usually characterized as lusty and promiscuous (in contrast to Diana's chastity)

7 *pampered animals / That rage in savage sensuality*

Perhaps this refers to pet monkeys, which were thought to have keen sexual appetites (see *Othello* 3.3.407, "hot as monkeys") or perhaps to well-fed horses (see *King Lear* 4.5.121 where the "soilèd horse" is said to be one of the animals that "goes to 't with a . . . riotous appetite").

Claudio

Not to be married,
proven Not to knit my soul to an approvèd° wanton.

Leonato

experience Dear my lord, if you in your own proof°
Have vanquished the resistance of her youth
And made defeat of her virginity—

Claudio

had intercourse with I know what you would say: if I have known° her,
You will say she did embrace me as a husband,
And so extenuate the forehand sin.[1]
No, Leonato,
coarse; inappropriate I never tempted her with word too large°
But, as a brother to his sister, showed
proper Bashful sincerity and comely° love.

Hero

And seemed I ever otherwise to you?

Claudio

Out on thee, seeming![2] I will write against it.[3]
You seem to me as Dian in her orb,[4]
As chaste as is the bud ere it be blown.[5]
passion But you are more intemperate in your blood°
Than Venus,[6] or those pampered animals
That rage in savage sensuality.[7]

Hero

wildly Is my lord well, that he doth speak so wide?°

Leonato

Sweet Prince, why speak not you?

Don Pedro

What should I speak?
I stand dishonored, that have gone about
prostitute To link my dear friend to a common stale.°

1 *True?*

Hero is reacting to Don John's *true* in line 65.

2 *catechizing*

Questioning. The catechism is the name for the series of questions and answers used to acquaint children with church doctrine. Hero and Claudio's ensuing dialogue may allude specifically to the catechism of the Anglican Book of Common Prayer, which begins, "What is your name?"

3 *To make you answer truly to your name.*

To make you admit that you are what I have termed you (i.e., a *stale*, line 63). In this dialogue, Hero is berated for not living up to her given name, which generally means a figure of virtue (*O Hero, what a Hero hadst thou been*, 4.1.98). The name also alludes to Hero, the faithful female lover of Leander, from Marlowe's *Hero and Leander* (1598). Benedick recalls this legend (5.2.24–25). Other characters have speaking names as well: Don John and Don Pedro allude to historical figures; Beatrice means "she who blesses," Benedick, "he who is blessed" (see page 14 of **Introduction to *Much Ado About Nothing***). Borachio (from the Spanish *borracho*, "drunk") says he will reveal all to Conrade, *like a true drunkard* (3.3.96). A *dogberry* is a female cornel, a common hedgerow bush used for medicinal purposes; Verges, the headborough or parish officer, is a form of *verjuice*, the acidic juice of sour fruit.

4 *that can Hero! / Hero itself can blot out Hero's virtue*

Hero can do that! Hero herself can cancel her name's link to virtue (that derives from the story of Hero and Leander).

Leonato

merely Are these things spoken, or do I but° dream?

Don John

Sir, they are spoken, and these things are true.

Benedick

This looks not like a nuptial.

Hero

True?[1] O God!

Claudio

Leonato, stand I here?
Is this the Prince? Is this the Prince's brother?
Is this face Hero's? Are our eyes our own?

Leonato

All this is so, but what of this, my lord?

Claudio

put Let me but move° one question to your daughter,
natural And by that fatherly and kindly° power
That you have in her, bid her answer truly.

Leonato

[*to* **Hero**] I charge thee do so, as thou art my child.

Hero

Oh, God defend me! How am I beset!
—What kind of catechizing[2] call you this?

Claudio

To make you answer truly to your name.[3]

Hero

Is it not Hero? Who can blot that name
criticism With any just reproach?°

Claudio

Marry, that can Hero!
Hero itself can blot out Hero's virtue.[4]
last night What man was he talked with you yesternight°
Out at your window betwixt twelve and one?

1 *much misgovernment*

Great misconduct

2 *gates of love*

I.e., the senses (especially the eyes)

Now, if you are a maid, answer to this.

Hero

I talked with no man at that hour, my lord.

Don Pedro

Why, then are you no maiden.—Leonato,
I am sorry you must hear. Upon mine honor,
wronged Myself, my brother, and this grievèd° count
Did see her, hear her, at that hour last night
Talk with a ruffian at her chamber window,
audacious Who hath indeed, most like a liberal° villain,
Confessed the vile encounters they have had
A thousand times in secret.

Don John

Fie, fie, they are not to be named, my lord,
Not to be spoke of!
There is not chastity enough in language
Without offense to utter them.—Thus, pretty lady,
I am sorry for thy much misgovernment. [1]

Claudio

O Hero, what a hero hadst thou been
beauty If half thy outward graces° had been placed
About thy thoughts and counsels of thy heart!
But fare thee well, most foul, most fair! Farewell,
Thou pure impiety and impious purity.
Because of For° thee I'll lock up all the gates of love,[2]
suspicion And on my eyelids shall conjecture° hang
To turn all beauty into thoughts of harm,
i.e., beauty / attractive And never shall it° more be gracious.°

Leonato

Hath no man's dagger here a point for me?

[**Hero** *swoons.*]

1 *printed in her blood*

(1) revealed by her blush; (2) determined by the innate inconstancy of women

Beatrice

Why Why, how now, cousin! Wherefore° sink you down?

Don John

Come, let us go. These things, come thus to light,
vitality Smother her spirits° up.

[**Don Pedro**, **Don John**, *and* **Claudio** *exit.*]

Benedick

How doth the lady?

Beatrice

Dead, I think.—Help, uncle!
—Hero, why, Hero! —Uncle! Signior Benedick! Friar!

Leonato

O Fate, take not away thy heavy hand!
Death is the fairest cover for her shame
That may be wished for.

Beatrice

How now, cousin Hero!

[**Hero** *moves.*]

Friar Francis

[*to* **Hero**] Have comfort, lady.

Leonato

[*to* **Hero**] Dost thou look up?

Friar Francis

why Yea, wherefore° should she not?

Leonato

Wherefore? Why, doth not every earthly thing
Cry shame upon her? Could she here deny
The story that is printed in her blood?[1]
open —Do not live, Hero; do not ope° thine eyes,
For, did I think thou wouldst not quickly die,
Thought I thy spirits were stronger than thy shames,

1 *Chid I for that at frugal nature's frame?*

Did I for that reason (i.e., having only been granted a single child) complain against stingy nature's plan?

2 *smirchèd thus*

I.e., stained as you have been

3 *That I myself was to myself not mine*

That I cared not at all for myself

4 *season give / To*

Keep from rotting; make appealing. Salt was used for seasoning and preserving meat as well as for embalming.

5 *attired in wonder*

Bewildered (literally, "dressed in amazement")

6 *barred up*

Reinforced

i.e., heels Myself would, on the rearward° of reproaches,
Strike at thy life. Grieved I I had but one?
Chid I for that at frugal nature's frame?[1]
in Oh, one too much by° thee! Why had I one?
Why ever wast thou lovely in my eyes?
Why had I not with charitable hand
child Took up a beggar's issue° at my gates,
soiled Who, smirchèd thus,[2] and mired° with infamy,
I might have said, "No part of it is mine;
This shame derives itself from unknown loins"?
But mine, and mine I loved, and mine I praised,
of And mine that I was proud on,° mine so much
That I myself was to myself not mine,[3]
Valuing of her. Why, she—oh, she is fall'n
Into a pit of ink, that the wide sea
Hath drops too few to wash her clean again
And salt too little which may season give
To[4] her foul tainted flesh!

Benedick

Sir, sir, be patient.
For my part, I am so attired in wonder[5]
I know not what to say.

Beatrice

slandered Oh, on my soul, my cousin is belied!°

Benedick

Lady, were you her bedfellow last night?

Beatrice

No, truly not, although until last night
I have this twelvemonth been her bedfellow.

Leonato

i.e., the accusation Confirmed, confirmed! Oh, that° is stronger made
already Which was before° barred up[6] with ribs of iron!

1 *given way unto this course of fortune, / By noting of the lady*

Allowed these events to pass so that I could watch (or because I was watching) Hero

2 *blushing apparitions / To start into her face, a thousand innocent shames / In angel whiteness beat away those blushes*

Hero has alternately blushed and paled. The Friar's description portrays the changes in her face as a battle between sin and innocence that innocence wins.

3 *a fire / To burn the errors*

The slanders would be burned as if they were people guilty of heresy.

4 *Which with experimental seal doth warrant / The tenor of my book*

Which have validated in practice the substance of my studies (*tenor of my book*)

5 *Thou see'st that all the grace that she hath left / Is that she will not add to her damnation / A sin of perjury.*

You can see that the only virtue she has left is that she won't add lying (*perjury*) to her list of sins.

Would the two Princes lie and Claudio lie,
Who loved her so that, speaking of her foulness,
Get away Washed it with tears? Hence° from her. Let her die.

Friar Francis

Hear me a little,
For I have only been silent so long,
And given way unto this course of fortune,
By noting of the lady.[1] I have marked
A thousand blushing apparitions
rush To start° into her face, a thousand innocent shames
In angel whiteness beat away those blushes,[2]
And in her eye there hath appeared a fire
To burn the errors[3] that these Princes hold
Against her maiden truth. Call me a fool,
intuition Trust not my reading° nor my observations,
Which with experimental seal doth warrant
The tenor of my book;[4] trust not my age,
position / theology My reverence,° calling, nor divinity,°
If this sweet lady lie not guiltless here
Under some biting error.

Leonato

Friar, it cannot be.
Thou see'st that all the grace that she hath left
Is that she will not add to her damnation
A sin of perjury.[5] She not denies it.
Why seek'st thou then to cover with excuse
true That which appears in proper° nakedness?

Friar Francis

Lady, what man is he you are accused of?

Hero

They know that do accuse me. I know none.
If I know more of any man alive

1 *Prove you*

If you prove

2 *have the very bent of*

Are totally inclined to (the image is of a bow fully drawn)

3 *Whose spirits toil in frame of*

Who expends all his energy in devising

4 *To quit me of them throughly*

Thoroughly to get my revenge on them

5 *Your daughter here the Princes left for dead.*

The Quarto reads "the princesse (left for dead)," which could be read as a convoluted appositive referring to Hero; nonetheless "princesse" is a common spelling of the plural of "prince," and the fact that Hero is not a princess, coupled with the repeated use of the term "Princes" for Don Pedro and Claudio (4.1.150, 161, and 183), makes it virtually certain that the line should be understood, as the 18th-century editor Theobald first noted, as meaning the two "Princes" believed Hero was dead.

allow Than that which maiden modesty doth warrant,°
Let all my sins lack mercy!—O my father,
Prove you [1] that any man with me conversed
inappropriate At hours unmeet,° or that I yesternight
exchange Maintained the change° of words with any creature,
Disown Refuse° me, hate me, torture me to death!

Friar Francis

misunderstanding There is some strange misprision° in the Princes.

Benedick

Two of them have the very bent of [2] honor,
judgment And if their wisdoms° be misled in this,
i.e., cause The practice° of it lives in John the bastard,
Whose spirits toil in frame of [3] villainies.

Leonato

I know not. If they speak but truth of her,
These hands shall tear her; if they wrong her honor,
The proudest of them shall well hear of it.
Time hath not yet so dried this blood of mine,
creativity Nor age so eat up my invention,°
wealth Nor fortune made such havoc of my means,°
robbed Nor my bad life reft° me so much of friends,
manner But they shall find, awaked in such a kind,°
cunning Both strength of limb and policy° of mind,
Ability in means and choice of friends,
To quit me of them throughly.[4]

Friar Francis

Pause awhile
And let my counsel sway you in this case.
Your daughter here the Princes left for dead.[5]
at home; inside Let her awhile be secretly kept in°
announce And publish° it that she is dead indeed.

1 *mourning ostentation*

Public display of grief

2 *on this travail look for greater birth*

I.e. from this effort I expect better results (than pity). *Travail* can mean "labor" both in the sense of "work" and the process of childbirth but also was indistinguishable from "travel," which is suggested by *course* in line 210.

3 *what we have we prize not to the worth*

We do not appreciate the full value of what we have.

4 *rack*

Exaggerate; strain torturously (as if on a *rack*, an instrument of torture)

5 *study of imagination*

I.e., deepest thoughts

6 *interest in his liver*

A claim upon his emotions. The liver, rather than the heart, was believed to be the source of passion and love.

Maintain a mourning ostentation,[1]
burial vault And on your family's old monument°
Hang mournful epitaphs and do all rites
That appertain unto a burial.

Leonato

from What shall become of° this? What will this do?

Friar Francis

carried out Marry, this, well carried,° shall on her behalf
pity Change slander to remorse.° That is some good.
But not for that dream I on this strange course,
But on this travail look for greater birth.[2]
She, dying, as it must be so maintained,
Upon the instant that she was accused,
Shall be lamented, pitied, and excused
By Of° every hearer. For it so falls out
That what we have we prize not to the worth[3]
Whiles we enjoy it, but being lacked and lost,
Why then we rack[4] the value, then we find
The virtue that possession would not show us
Whiles it was ours. So will it fare with Claudio.
from the impact of When he shall hear she died upon° his words,
image Th' idea° of her life shall sweetly creep
Into his study of imagination,[5]
aspect And every lovely organ° of her life
clothing Shall come apparelled in more precious habit,°
More moving, delicate, and full of life,
scope of vision Into the eye and prospect° of his soul
Than when she lived indeed. Then shall he mourn,
If ever love had interest in his liver,[6]
And wish he had not so accusèd her,
No, though he thought his accusation true.
succeeding events Let this be so, and doubt not but success°

1 *I can lay it down in likelihood*

I can predict

2 *if all aim but this be leveled false*

I.e., even if everything fails but the rumor of her death

3 *wonder of*

Speculation about

4 *Out of*

Away from

5 *Being that I flow in*

Because I am overwhelmed by

6 *to strange sores strangely they strain the cure*

Desperate diseases require desperate remedies (proverbial).

outcome Will fashion the event° in better shape
Than I can lay it down in likelihood.[1]
plans But if all aim° but this be leveled false,[2]
The supposition of the lady's death
Will quench the wonder of[3] her infamy.
turn out And if it sort° not well, you may conceal her,
As best befits her wounded reputation,
cloistered In some reclusive° and religious life,
insults Out of[4] all eyes, tongues, minds, and injuries.°

Benedick

Signior Leonato, let the Friar advise you;
intimate friendship And though you know my inwardness° and love
Is very much unto the Prince and Claudio,
Yet, by mine honor, I will deal in this
As secretly and justly as your soul
Should with your body.

Leonato

Being that I flow in[5] grief,
thread The smallest twine° may lead me.

Friar Francis

Immediately 'Tis well consented. Presently° away,
For to strange sores strangely they strain the cure.[6]
—Come, lady; die to live. This wedding day
postponed Perhaps is but prolonged.° Have patience and endure.

[*All but* **Benedick** *and* **Beatrice**] *exit.*

Benedick

Lady Beatrice, have you wept all this while?

Beatrice

Yea, and I will weep awhile longer.

Benedick

I will not desire that.

1 *By my sword*

A gentleman's oath

2 *and eat it*

And end up having to eat your words; Benedick's wordplay in lines 272–273 takes it as "eat your sword."

Beatrice

i.e., of my own will You have no reason. I do it freely.°

Benedick

Surely I do believe your fair cousin is wronged.

Beatrice

Ah, how much might the man deserve of me that would right° her! *avenge*

Benedick

Is there any way to show such friendship?

Beatrice

direct A very even° way, but no such friend.

Benedick

May a man do it?

Beatrice

duty It is a man's office,° but not yours.

Benedick

I do love nothing in the world so well as you. Is not that strange?

Beatrice

As strange as the thing I know not. It were as possible for me to say I loved nothing so well as you, but believe me not, and yet I lie not. I confess nothing, nor I deny nothing. I am sorry for my cousin.

Benedick

By my sword,[1] Beatrice, thou lovest me.

Beatrice

Do not swear and eat it.[2]

Benedick

I will swear by it that you love me, and I will make him eat it that says I love not you.

Beatrice

Will you not eat your word?

1 *God forgive me*

Either for nearly violating the convention that the man would be the first to declare his love, or for thinking of love at all at this apparently tragic time

2 *You have stayed me in a happy hour.*

You have stopped me just in time.

3 *Kill Claudio.*

(See Longer Note on page 303.)

4 *I am gone, though I am here.*

I.e., even if you forcibly hold me here, I am gone in spirit.

Benedick

insist With no sauce that can be devised to it. I protest° I love thee.

Beatrice

Why then, God forgive me.[1]

Benedick

What offense, sweet Beatrice?

Beatrice

stopped You have stayed° me in a happy hour.[2] I was about to protest I loved you.

Benedick

And do it with all thy heart.

Beatrice

object I love you with so much of my heart that none is left to protest.°

Benedick

Come; bid me do anything for thee.

Beatrice

Kill Claudio.[3]

Benedick

Ha! Not for the wide world.

Beatrice

refuse You kill me to deny° it. Farewell. [*begins to leave*]

Benedick

Wait [*stopping her*] Tarry,° sweet Beatrice.

Beatrice

I am gone, though I am here.[4] There is no love in you. Nay, I pray you let me go.

Benedick

Beatrice—

Beatrice

In faith, I will go.

1 *Is 'a not approved in the height a villain*

Is he not thoroughly proven to be a villain

2 *bear her in hand*

I.e., lead her on

3 *A proper saying!*

Sarcastically, "quite the story!"

4 *a goodly count*

(1) a fine excuse for a nobleman; (2) a likely story; (3) a telling accusation

5 *Count Comfect*

Count Candy, i.e., a nobleman of no substance

Benedick

We'll be friends first.

Beatrice

You dare easier be friends with me than fight with mine enemy.

Benedick

Is Claudio thine enemy?

Beatrice

he

Is 'a° not approved in the height a villain,[1] that hath slandered, scorned, dishonored my kinswoman? Oh, that I were a man! What, bear her in hand[2] until they come to take hands and then, with public accusation, uncovered° slander, unmitigated rancor—O God, that I were a man! I would eat his heart in the marketplace.

bald-faced; blatant

Benedick

Hear me, Beatrice—

Beatrice

Talk with a man out at a window! A proper saying![3]

Benedick

Nay, but Beatrice—

Beatrice

Sweet Hero, she is wronged; she is slandered; she is undone.

Benedick

Beat—

Beatrice

counts

Princes and counties!° Surely a princely testimony, a goodly count,[4] Count Comfect,[5] a sweet gallant surely! Oh, that I were a man for his sake, or that I had any friend would be a man for my sake! But manhood is melted into curtsies, valor into compliment,° and men are only turned into tongue,° and trim° ones

flattery

talkers / glib

1 *He is now as valiant as Hercules that only tells a lie and swears it.*

I.e., a man today can be considered as brave as Hercules if he simply tells a lie and then swears to its truth.

2 *render me a dear account*

Pay dearly (for his actions)

too. He is now as valiant as Hercules that only tells a lie and swears it.[1] I cannot be a man with° wishing, therefore I will die a woman with grieving.

by

Benedick

Tarry, good Beatrice; by this hand, I love thee.

Beatrice

Use it for my love some other way than swearing by it.

Benedick

Think you in your soul the Count Claudio hath wronged Hero?

Beatrice

Yea, as sure as I have a thought or a soul.

Benedick

Enough; I am engaged.° I will challenge him. I will kiss your hand, and so I leave you. By this hand, Claudio shall render me a dear account.[2] As you hear of me, so think of me. Go comfort your cousin. I must say she is dead, and so farewell. [*They exit separately.*]

pledged

1 in gowns

Black gowns, worn by the Sexton and the constables

2 *that am I and my partner*

Dogberry mistakes *malefactors* for "factors," which meant "agents" or "deputies."

3 *sirrah*

A term of address, often used contemptuously, to refer to those of lesser social rank, thus provoking a reaction from Conrade

Act 4, Scene 2

*Enter the constables [**Dogberry** and **Verges**] and the [**Sexton**], in gowns,*[1] *[with the watch, **Conrade** and]* **Borachio**.

Dogberry

(error for "assembly") Is our whole dissembly° appeared?

Verges

Oh, a stool and a cushion for the sexton.

*[A stool is brought forward, and the **Sexton** sits.]*

Sexton

Which be the malefactors?

Dogberry

Marry, that am I and my partner.[2]

Verges

(error for "commission") Nay, that's certain; we have the exhibition° to examine.

Sexton

But which are the offenders that are to be examined? Let them come before Master Constable.

Dogberry

Yea, marry, let them come before me.

*[**Conrade** and **Borachio** are pushed forward.]*

—What is your name, friend?

Borachio

Borachio.

Dogberry

*[to the **Sexton**]* Pray, write down "Borachio."—Yours, sirrah?[3]

Conrade

I am a gentleman, sir, and my name is Conrade.

Dogberry

Write down "Master Gentleman Conrade."—Masters, do you serve God?

1 *but God should go before*

But that God should have priority over

2 *go a bout with*

I.e., contend with

3 *they are both in a tale*

I.e., their stories agree.

4 *you go not the way*

You are not following the proper procedures.

5 *eftest*

Quickest; best (perhaps his error for "aptest" or "deftest")

6 *perjury*

His error for "treachery," as is, perhaps, *burglary* in line 45

Conrade and Borachio

Yea, sir, we hope.

Dogberry

Write down that they hope they serve God; and write "God" first, for God defend° but God should go before[1] such villains!—Masters, it is proved already that you are little better than false knaves, and it will go near to be thought so shortly. How answer you for yourselves?

forbid

Conrade

Marry, sir, we say we are none.

Dogberry

A marvelous witty° fellow, I assure you, but I will go a bout with[2] him.—Come you hither, sirrah, a word in your ear. Sir, I say to you it is thought you are false knaves.

clever

Borachio

Sir, I say to you we are none.

Dogberry

Well, stand aside.—'Fore God, they are both in a tale.[3] Have you writ down that they are none?

Sexton

Master Constable, you go not the way[4] to examine. You must call forth the watch that are their accusers.

Dogberry

Yea, marry, that's the eftest[5] way.—Let the watch come forth.—Masters, I charge you in the Prince's name, accuse these men.

First Watchman

This man said, sir, that Don John, the Prince's brother, was a villain.

Dogberry

[*to* **Sexton**] Write down "Prince John a villain."—Why, this is flat perjury,[6] to call a prince's brother "villain."

1 *by mass*

A mild oath (by the mass)

2 *upon his words*

On the strength of his word

Borachio

Master Constable—

Dogberry

Pray thee, fellow, peace. I do not like thy look, I promise thee.

Sexton

[*to* **Watchmen**] What heard you him say else?

Seacole

Marry, that he had received a thousand ducats of Don John for accusing the lady Hero wrongfully.

Dogberry

Flat-out Flat° burglary as ever was committed.

Verges

Yea, by mass,[1] that it is.

Sexton

What else, fellow?

First Watchman

And that Count Claudio did mean upon his words[2] to disgrace Hero before the whole assembly, and not marry her.

Dogberry

[*to* **Borachio**] O villain! Thou wilt be condemned into everlasting redemption° for this. *(error for "damnation")*

Sexton

What else?

First Watchman

This is all.

Sexton

And this is more, masters, than you can deny. Prince John is this morning secretly stolen away. Hero was in this manner accused, in this very manner refused, and upon the grief of this, suddenly died.—Master Constable, let these men be bound and brought to

1 *opinioned*

Dogberry's error for "pinioned," i.e., restrained

2 *coxcomb*

"Fool;" literally the name for a fool's cap

3 *as pretty a piece of flesh*

As handsome a specimen

4 *go to*

An intensifier, something like "I assure you"

5 *losses*

Even *losses* can be seen as desirable in Dogberry's self-satisfied catalogue of his fine qualities, no doubt as they point to his former wealth, and he still has enough to afford *two gowns* (line 80).

Leonato's. I will go before and show him their examination. [*He exits.*]

Dogberry

Come, let them be opinioned.[1]

Verges

Let them be in the hands—

Conrade

Off, coxcomb![2]

Dogberry

God save God's° my life, where's the sexton? Let him write down the Prince's officer "coxcomb." Come, bind them. [**Conrade** *and* **Borachio** *are held by the watchmen.*]

wicked —Thou naughty° varlet!

Conrade

Away! You are an ass; you are an ass!

Dogberry

(error for "respect") Dost thou not suspect° my place? Dost thou not

i.e., the sexton suspect my years?—Oh, that he° were here to write me down "an ass"!—But masters, remember that I am an ass, though it be not written down, yet forget not that I am an ass.—No, thou villain, thou art full of

(error for "impiety") piety,° as shall be proved upon thee by good witness. I am a wise fellow and, which is more, an officer and, which is more, a householder and, which is more, as pretty a piece of flesh[3] as any is in Messina, and one that knows the law, go to,[4] and a rich fellow enough, go to, and a fellow that hath had losses,[5] and one that hath two gowns and everything handsome about him.—Bring him away.—Oh, that I had been writ down an ass! [*They*] *exit.*

1 *second*

Assist (as in a duel); reinforce

2 *Measure his woe the length and breadth of mine, / And let it answer every strain for strain*

I.e., compare his woe to mine, and see if it can match mine pang for pang.

3 *stroke his beard . . . cry "hem"*

Stroking the beard and clearing the throat were taken as the forerunners of dull and clichéd speeches.

4 *candle-wasters*

I.e., people who stay up late to study; those who would offer precepts learned from books as a remedy for felt grief

Act 5, Scene 1

Enter **Leonato** *and* [**Antonio**,] *his brother.*

Antonio

If you go on thus you will kill yourself,
And 'tis not wisdom thus to second[1] grief
Against yourself.

Leonato

I pray thee, cease thy counsel,
Which falls into mine ears as profitless
As water in a sieve. Give not me counsel,
Nor let no comforter delight mine ear
compare But such a one whose wrongs do suit° with mine.
Bring me a father that so loved his child,
in Whose joy of° her is overwhelmed like mine,
And bid him speak of patience.
Measure his woe the length and breadth of mine,
And let it answer every strain for strain,[2]
As thus for thus and such a grief for such,
contour In every lineament,° branch, shape, and form.
If such a one will smile and stroke his beard,
be gone Bid sorrow wag,° cry "hem"[3] when he should groan,
Mend / stupefied Patch° grief with proverbs, make misfortune drunk°
then With candle-wasters,[4] bring him yet° to me,
And I of him will gather patience.
But there is no such man. For, brother, men
Can counsel and speak comfort to that grief
Which they themselves not feel, but, tasting it,
Their counsel turns to passion, which before
maxims as Would give preceptial° med'cine to rage,
Tie up Fetter° strong madness in a silken thread,
Subdue / i.e., talk Charm° ache with air,° and agony with words.

1 *writ the style of gods / And made a push at chance and sufferance*

Expressed a godlike patience, scoffing in the face of misfortune and suffering

2 *Good e'en*

Good evening (could be used as an address anytime after noon)

3 *Hear you*

Will you hear me

duty No, no, 'tis all men's office° to speak patience
suffer To those that wring° under the load of sorrow,
strength / ability But no man's virtue° nor sufficiency°
moralistic To be so moral° when he shall endure
The like himself. Therefore give me no counsel.
advice My griefs cry louder than advertisement.°

Antonio

not at all Therein do men from children nothing° differ.

Leonato

be quiet I pray thee, peace.° I will be flesh and blood,
For there was never yet philosopher
That could endure the toothache patiently,
However much However° they have writ the style of gods
And made a push at chance and sufferance.[1]

Antonio

direct Yet bend° not all the harm upon yourself.
Make those that do offend you suffer too.

Leonato

There thou speak'st reason. Nay, I will do so.
My soul doth tell me Hero is belied,
And that shall Claudio know; so shall the Prince
And all of them that thus dishonor her.

Enter [**Don Pedro**] *and* **Claudio**.

Antonio

Here comes the Prince and Claudio hastily.

Don Pedro

Good e'en,[2] good e'en.

Claudio

Good day to both of you.

Leonato

Hear you,[3] my lords—

1 *all is one*

It's all the same; it doesn't matter.

2 *Some of us would lie low*

I.e., Don Pedro and Claudio would be slain.

3 *thou*

Leonato uses the familiar *thou* to show his disgust with Claudio, unlike his respectful *you* (lines 48–49) to the Prince, even though there too he is obviously upset.

4 *my hand meant nothing to*

I.e., my hand had no intention of drawing

5 *Tush*

A dismissive exclamation (as at 3.3.112 and 5.4.44)

6 *lay my reverence by*

Ignore the fact of my age

7 *trial of a man*

Trial of manhood, i.e., a duel

8 *she lies buried*

Not literally true, of course, as Hero is only hidden away. Leonato and Antonio's rage has consequently been dismissed as excessive and comical playacting. But the accusation of infidelity has destroyed Hero's reputation and her chances for marriage. Leonato redirects his paternal frustration and anger from Hero to men he can hold responsible.

Don Pedro

We have some haste, Leonato.

Leonato

Some haste, my lord? Well, fare you well, my lord.
Are you so hasty now? Well, all is one.[1]

Don Pedro

Nay, do not quarrel with us, good old man.

Antonio

If he could right himself with quarreling,
Some of us would lie low.[2]

Claudio

Who wrongs him?

Leonato

Marry, thou dost wrong me, thou dissembler, thou.[3]
Nay, never lay thy hand upon thy sword.
I fear thee not.

Claudio

curse Marry, beshrew° my hand
If it should give your age such cause of fear.
In faith, my hand meant nothing to[4] my sword.

Leonato

sneer Tush,[5] tush, man, never fleer° and jest at me!
I speak not like a dotard nor a fool,
As under privilege of age to brag
What I have done being young, or what would do
face Were I not old. Know, Claudio, to thy head,°
Thou hast so wronged mine innocent child and me
That I am forced to lay my reverence by,[6]
And, with gray hairs and bruise of many days,
Do challenge thee to trial of a man.[7]
I say thou hast belied mine innocent child.
Thy slander hath gone through and through her heart,
And she lies buried[8] with her ancestors,

1 *nice fence*

Refined fencing skills (see note 3 below)

2 *Win me and wear me!*

I.e., if he should beat me, then he may brag about it (proverbial).

3 *foining fence*

Swordplay; *foining* indicates his contempt for the new, Italian fencing techniques that emphasized the sword point rather than the blade in the attack. A "foin" was a downward thrust.

4 *Content yourself.*

I.e., stay out of it.

Oh, in a tomb where never scandal slept
created Save this of hers, framed° by thy villainy.

Claudio

My villainy?

Leonato

Thine, Claudio, thine, I say.

Don Pedro

You say not right, old man.

Leonato

My lord, my lord,
I'll prove it on his body if he dare,
Despite his nice fence[1] and his active practice,
virility His May of youth and bloom of lustihood.°

Claudio

Away! I will not have to do with you.

Leonato

cast aside Canst thou so doff° me? Thou hast killed my child.
If thou kill'st me, boy, thou shalt kill a man.

Antonio

He shall kill two of us, and men indeed,
But that's no matter. Let him kill one first.
duel with Win me and wear me![2] Let him answer° me.
—Come, follow me, boy. Come, sir boy; come, follow me.
Sir boy, I'll whip you from your foining fence.[3]
Nay, as I am a gentleman, I will.

Leonato

Brother—

Antonio

Content yourself.[4] God knows I loved my niece,
And she is dead, slandered to death by villains
That dare as well answer a man indeed
As I dare take a serpent by the tongue.
fools / knaves Boys, apes,° braggarts, jacks,° milksops!

1 *scruple*

A unit of measurement used by apothecaries, equal to one twenty-fourth of an ounce

2 *Scambling, outfacing, fashion-monging*

Pushy, rude, trendy

3 *show outward hideousness*

Look frightening

4 *this is all*

I.e., it is just mere show.

Leonato

Brother Anthony—

Antonio

Hold you content. What, man! I know them, yea,
And what they weigh, even to the utmost scruple:[1]
Scambling, outfacing, fashion-monging[2] boys
cheat / mock / disparage That lie and cog° and flout,° deprave° and slander,
ostentatiously dressed Go anticly° and show outward hideousness,[3]
threatening And speak off half a dozen dang'rous° words
dared How they might hurt their enemies, if they durst,°
And this is all.[4]

Leonato

But brother Anthony—

Antonio

Come, 'tis no matter.
Do not you meddle. Let me deal in this.

Don Pedro

test Gentlemen both, we will not wake° your patience.
My heart is sorry for your daughter's death,
But, on my honor, she was charged with nothing
But what was true and very full of proof.

Leonato

My lord, my lord—

Don Pedro

I will not hear you.

Leonato

No? Come, brother; away! I will be heard.

Antonio

And shall, or some of us will smart for it.

Both [brothers] exit.

Enter **Benedick**.

1 *We had liked to have had*

We almost had

2 *false quarrel*

Unwarranted fight

3 *beside their wit*

I.e., out of their minds

4 *draw, as we do the minstrels*

Claudio tries to defuse Benedick's menacing suggestion that his wit is in his scabbard (i.e., he is ready to draw his sword), and asks him to *draw* his wit only as musicians draw their bows across the strings of their instruments (or their instruments from their cases), in order to give pleasure.

Don Pedro

See; see: here comes the man we went to seek.

Claudio

Now, signior, what news?

Benedick

[*to* **Don Pedro**] Good day, my lord.

Don Pedro

Welcome, signior. You are almost come to part almost a fray.

Claudio

We had liked to have had[1] our two noses snapped off with° two old men without teeth.

by

Don Pedro

Leonato and his brother. What think'st thou? Had we fought, I doubt° we should have been too young for them.

suspect

Benedick

In a false quarrel[2] there is no true valor. I came to seek you both.

Claudio

We have been up and down to seek thee, for we are high-proof° melancholy and would fain° have it beaten away. Wilt thou use thy wit?

i.e., extremely / gladly

Benedick

It is in my scabbard. Shall I draw it?

Don Pedro

Dost thou wear thy wit by thy side?

Claudio

Never any did so, though very many have been beside their wit.[3] I will bid thee draw, as we do the minstrels:[4] draw to pleasure us.

Don Pedro

As I am an honest man, he looks pale.—Art thou sick or angry?

1 *care killed a cat*

A proverbial expression (*care* meaning "worry; anxiety; grief")

2 *in the career*

I.e., head-on (the metaphor is from jousting, referring to knights meeting at full gallop)

3 *This last was broke 'cross.*

I.e., this last (*staff*, i.e., remark) was poorly wielded. A lance broken across the middle (as it would if not carried straight) would have been misused, either out of incompetence or cowardice. Claudio does not take seriously Benedick's warning not to mock him.

4 *he knows how to turn his girdle*

I.e., he knows he must accept the insult.

5 *Do me right*

Give me satisfaction by accepting this challenge.

6 *a feast*

Don Pedro deliberately misunderstands Claudio's comment (taking *cheer* as entertainment).

7 *a calf's head and a capon*

Dishes served at feast, whose names also serve to deride Benedick: *calf's head* is slang for "fool;" a *capon* is a castrated rooster and therefore meant "eunuch." *Woodcock* has the same double function, meaning "simpleton" as well as referring to a game bird.

Claudio

So what [*to* **Benedick**] What? Courage, man! What° though care
courage; spirit killed a cat?[1] Thou hast mettle° enough in thee to kill care.

Benedick

if / aim Sir, I shall meet your wit in the career,[2] an° you charge°
target; topic it against me. I pray you, choose another subject.°

Claudio

lance [*to* **Don Pedro**] Nay, then, give him another staff.° This
last was broke 'cross.[3]

Don Pedro

By this light, he changes more and more. I think he be angry indeed.

Claudio

If he be, he knows how to turn his girdle.[4]

Benedick

Shall I speak a word in your ear?

Claudio

protect God bless° me from a challenge!

Benedick

[*to* **Claudio**] You are a villain. I jest not. I will make it
whichever weapon good how you dare, with what° you dare, and when
proclaim you dare. Do me right,[5] or I will protest° your coward-
ice. You have killed a sweet lady, and her death shall fall heavy on you. Let me hear from you.

Claudio

Very well Well.° I will meet you so I may have good cheer.

Don Pedro

What? A feast,[6] a feast?

Claudio

invited I' faith, I thank him. He hath bid° me to a calf's head
and a capon,[7] the which if I do not carve most
skillfully / worthless curiously,° say my knife's naught.° Shall I not find a
woodcock too?

1 *ambles*

I.e., goes slowly and aimlessly (suggesting that Claudio is not quick witted)

2 *a wise gentleman*

A sarcastic epithet along the lines of "old fool"

3 *tongues*

Command of several languages

4 *an if*

If

5 *God saw him when he was hid in the garden*

After eating the forbidden fruit, Adam and Eve attempt to hide themselves from God (Genesis 3:8).

6 *the savage bull's horns on the sensible Benedick's head? / Yea, and text underneath: "Here dwells Benedick the married man"?*

Don Pedro and Claudio refer to Benedick's injunction to put the cuckold's horns on his head and have his picture painted on a sign if he were ever to fall in love and marry (1.1.229–234).

Benedick

Sir, your wit ambles[1] well; it goes easily.

Don Pedro

I'll tell thee how Beatrice praised thy wit the other day. I said thou hadst a fine wit. "True," said she, "a fine° little one." "No," said I, "a great wit." "Right," says she, "a great gross one." "Nay," said I, "a good wit." "Just,"° said she; "it hurts nobody." "Nay," said I, "the gentleman is wise." "Certain," said she, "a wise gentleman."[2] "Nay," said I, "he hath the tongues."[3] "That I believe," said she, "for he swore a thing to me on Monday night, which he forswore on Tuesday morning. There's a double° tongue; there's two tongues." Thus did she an hour together transshape° thy particular virtues. Yet at last she concluded, with a sigh, thou wast the proper'st° man in Italy.

i.e., thin; narrow
Exactly
deceitful
distort
finest

Claudio

For the which she wept heartily and said she cared not.

Don Pedro

Yea, that she did. But yet for all that, an if[4] she did not hate him deadly, she would love him dearly. The old man's daughter° told us all.

i.e., Hero

Claudio

All, all. And, moreover, God saw him when he was hid in the garden.[5]

Don Pedro

But when shall we set the savage bull's horns on the sensible Benedick's head?

Claudio

Yea, and text underneath: "Here dwells Benedick the married man"?[6]

1 *gossip-like humor*

I.e., chatty, smirking mood

2 *as braggarts do their blades*

I.e., by breaking their own swords so that they may boast their experience fighting without risking or doing harm

3 *discontinue your company*

Resign from your service

4 *goes in his doublet and hose and leaves off his wit*

I.e., shows himself ready to fight (by removing his cloak) but forgets to display his intelligence

5 *is then a giant to an ape, but then is an ape a doctor to such a man*

Seems a great man to a fool (*ape*), but in fact the fool is a great scholar compared with such a person

6 *Pluck up*

Pull yourself together.

Benedick

Fare you well, boy. You know my mind. I will leave you
crack now to your gossip-like humor.[1] You break° jests as
braggarts do their blades,[2] which, God be thanked,
kindnesses hurt not.—My lord, for your many courtesies° I thank
you. I must discontinue your company.[3] Your brother
the Bastard is fled from Messina. You have among you
killed a sweet and innocent lady. For my Lord Lack-
i.e., Claudio / (in a duel) beard° there, he and I shall meet,° and till then peace
be with him. *[He exits.]*

Don Pedro

He is in earnest.

Claudio

guarantee In most profound earnest, and, I'll warrant° you, for
the love of Beatrice.

Don Pedro

And hath challenged thee?

Claudio

Most sincerely.

Don Pedro

What a pretty thing man is when he goes in his doublet and hose and leaves off his wit![4]

Claudio

He is then a giant to an ape, but then is an ape a doctor
to such a man.[5]

Don Pedro

wait But soft° you; let me be. Pluck up,[6] my heart, and be
serious sad.° Did he not say my brother was fled?

*Enter constables [***Dogberry** *and* **Verges***, with the watch, and]* **Conrade** *and* **Borachio***.*

1 *reasons*

There is perhaps a weak joke here from the fact that *reasons* was pronounced similarly to "raisins," giving rise to a comic image of the scales of justice weighing *reasons* as a shopkeeper's scales would weigh dried fruit.

2 *looked to*

Dealt with

3 *Hearken after*

Ask about

4 *what you lay to their charge*

What are they charged with

5 *in his own division*

According to his (Dogberry's) own organizational scheme

6 *one meaning well suited*

I.e., just the one thought dressed up in various ways

7 *bound to your answer*

Forced to respond (and punning on the sense "tied up awaiting your trial")

8 *go no farther to mine answer*

Answer the question right now.

Dogberry

Come you, sir. If justice cannot tame you, she shall ne'er weigh more reasons[1] in her balance.° Nay, an° you be a cursing hypocrite, once,° you must be looked to.[2]

scales / if
in a word

Don Pedro

How now? Two of my brother's men bound! Borachio one!

Claudio

Hearken after[3] their offense, my lord.

Don Pedro

Officers, what offense have these men done?

Dogberry

Marry, sir, they have committed false report; moreover, they have spoken untruths; secondarily, they are slanders;° sixth and lastly, they have belied° a lady; thirdly, they have verified unjust things; and, to conclude, they are lying knaves.

i.e., slanderers / defamed

Don Pedro

First, I ask thee what they have done; thirdly, I ask thee what's their offense; sixth and lastly, why they are committed;° and, to conclude, what you lay to their charge.[4]

taken into custody

Claudio

Rightly reasoned, and in his own division,[5] and, by my troth,° there's one meaning well suited.[6]

faith

Don Pedro

[*to* **Borachio** *and* **Conrade**] Who have you offended, masters, that you are thus bound to your answer?[7] This learnèd constable is too cunning° to be understood. What's your offense?

clever

Borachio

Sweet Prince, let me go no farther to mine answer.[8]

1 *Do you hear me*

Hear me out.

2 *rare semblance that*

Remarkable form in which

Do you hear me,[1] and let this Count kill me. I have deceived even your very eyes. What your wisdoms could not discover, these shallow fools have brought to light, who in the night overheard me confessing to this man how Don John your brother incensed° me to slander the lady Hero, how you were brought into the orchard° and saw me court Margaret in Hero's garments, [*to* **Claudio**] how you disgraced her when you should marry her. My villainy they have upon record, which I had rather seal° with my death than repeat over to my shame. The lady is dead upon° mine and my master's false accusation. And, briefly, I desire nothing but the reward of a villain.

incensed: provoked
orchard: garden
seal: confirm; conclude
upon: as a consequence of

Don Pedro
[*to* **Claudio**] Runs not this speech like iron° through your blood?

iron: i.e., a sword

Claudio
I have drunk poison whiles he uttered it.

Don Pedro
[*to* **Borachio**] But did my brother set thee on to this?

Borachio
Yea, and paid me richly for the practice° of it.

practice: execution

Don Pedro
He is composed and framed° of treachery,
And fled he is upon this villainy.

framed: constructed

Claudio
Sweet Hero, now thy image doth appear
In the rare semblance that[2] I loved it first.

Dogberry
Come; bring away the plaintiffs.° By this time our sexton hath reformed° Signior Leonato of the matter. And, masters, do not forget to specify, when time and place shall serve, that I am an ass.

plaintiffs: (error for "defendants")
reformed: (error for "informed")

1 *nor I*

I.e., so did I (sin only *in mistaking*)

Verges
Here, here comes Master Signior Leonato, and the sexton too.

Enter **Leonato**, *his brother* [**Antonio**], *and the* **Sexton**.

Leonato
Which is the villain? Let me see his eyes
That, when I note another man like him,
I may avoid him. Which of these is he?

Borachio
If you would know your wronger, look on me.

Leonato
Art thou the slave that with thy breath hast killed
Mine innocent child?

Borachio
Yea, even I alone.

Leonato
slander No, not so, villain; thou beliest° thyself.
noble Here stand a pair of honorable° men—
A third is fled—that had a hand in it.
—I thank you, Princes, for my daughter's death.
Record it with your high and worthy deeds.
'Twas bravely done, if you bethink you of it.

Claudio
entreat I know not how to pray° your patience,
Yet I must speak. Choose your revenge yourself.
Subject Impose° me to what penance your invention
Can lay upon my sin. Yet sinned I not
But in mistaking.

Don Pedro
By my soul, nor I; [1]

1 *enjoin me to*

Impose upon me

2 *Can labor aught in sad invention*

Can work to write something appropriately somber

3 *an epitaph upon her tomb*

As the Friar suggested at 4.1.205

4 *heir to both of us*

Leonato overlooks Antonio's son (mentioned at 1.2.1–2), either to reinforce the fact that Claudio will be an heir, or because the earlier reference or this is merely a mistake.

5 *right*

Deserved treatment (but punning on marriage "rite")

6 *dispose / For henceforth of poor Claudio*

I.e., from here on you may deal with me as you see fit.

And yet to satisfy this good old man
I would bend under any heavy weight
That he'll enjoin me to.[1]

Leonato

I cannot bid you bid my daughter live—
That were impossible—but, I pray you both,
Inform Possess° the people in Messina here
How innocent she died. And, if your love
Can labor aught in sad invention,[2]
for her Hang her° an epitaph upon her tomb[3]
And sing it to her bones. Sing it tonight.
Tomorrow morning come you to my house,
And, since you could not be my son-in-law,
Be yet my nephew. My brother hath a daughter,
Almost the copy of my child that's dead,
And she alone is heir to both of us.[4]
Give her the right[5] you should have giv'n her cousin,
And so dies my revenge.

Claudio

O noble sir!
Your overkindness doth wring tears from me.
I do embrace your offer and dispose
For henceforth of poor Claudio.[6]

Leonato

Tomorrow then I will expect your coming.
wicked Tonight I take my leave. This naughty° man
Shall face to face be brought to Margaret,
complicit Who I believe was packed° in all this wrong,
Hired to it by your brother.

Borachio

No, by my soul, she was not,
Nor knew not what she did when she spoke to me,
But always hath been just and virtuous

1 *under white and black*

I.e., in writing

2 *he wears a key in his ear and a lock hanging by it*

Dogberry's interpretation of "wore a lock" (see 3.3.156 and note)

3 *thankful and reverent youth*

Dogberry's error for "gracious and reverend elder," i.e., generous and respected gentleman

4 *God save the foundation!*

This phrase was customarily used by beneficiaries to thank churches and other instutions for alms.

5 *which I beseech your Worship to correct yourself*

Whom I beg your Worship to punish yourself

of In anything that I do know by° her.

Dogberry

[*to* **Leonato**] Moreover, sir, which indeed is not under white and black,[1] this plaintiff° here, the offender, did call me "ass." I beseech you, let it be remembered in his punishment. And also the watch heard them talk of one Deformed. They say he wears a key in his ear and a lock hanging by it[2] and borrows money in God's name, the which he hath used so long and never paid° that now men grow hard-hearted and will lend nothing for God's sake. Pray you, examine him upon that point.

(error for "defendant")

repaid

Leonato

I thank thee for thy care and honest pains.

Dogberry

Your Worship speaks like a most thankful and reverent youth,[3] and I praise God for you.

Leonato

[*giving him money*] There's for thy pains.

Dogberry

God save the foundation![4]

Leonato

Go; I discharge thee of thy prisoner, and I thank thee.

Dogberry

I leave an arrant° knave with your Worship, which I beseech your Worship to correct yourself[5] for the example of others. God keep your Worship! I wish your Worship well. God restore you to health! I humbly give° you leave to depart, and if a merry meeting may be wished, God prohibit° it!—Come neighbor.

absolute

(error for "ask")

(error for "permit")

[**Dogberry** *and* **Verges** *exit.*]

Leonato

Until tomorrow morning, lords, farewell.

Antonio

Farewell, my lords. We look for you tomorrow.

Don Pedro

We will not fail.

Claudio

Tonight I'll mourn with Hero.

Leonato

[*to the* **Watchmen**] Bring you these fellows on.—We'll talk with Margaret,

How her acquaintance grew with this lewd° fellow.

worthless

They exit.

1 *come over it*

(1) outdo it; (2) climb over it, with a pun on *style/stile* (steps for climbing over a fence or wall)

2 *come over*

Margaret takes Benedick's pun in a bawdy sense: lie on (in the sexual act).

3 *below stairs*

I.e., in the servants' quarters

4 *fencer's foils*

Which, as they are for practice, have blunted tips

5 *I give thee the bucklers.*

I.e., I surrender; *bucklers* were small shields with spikes (*pikes*) in the center.

6 *we have bucklers*

Margaret bawdily associates *bucklers* with the thighs protecting the genitalia.

7 *put in the pikes with a vice*

More bawdy joking: screw in the spikes (obviously phallic).

8 *hath legs*

I.e., can walk (but continuing the joke in line 15)

Act 5, Scene 2

Enter **Benedick** *and* **Margaret**.

Benedick

Pray thee, sweet Mistress Margaret, deserve well at my hands by helping me to the speech of Beatrice.

Margaret

Will you then write me a sonnet in praise of my beauty?

Benedick

In so high a style, Margaret, that no man living shall come over it,[1] for in most comely truth thou deservest it.

Margaret

To have no man come over[2] me? Why, shall I always keep° below stairs?[3]

remain

Benedick

Thy wit is as quick as the greyhound's mouth; it catches.°

bites

Margaret

And yours as blunt as the fencer's foils,[4] which hit but hurt not.

Benedick

A most manly wit, Margaret; it will not hurt a woman. And so, I pray thee, call Beatrice. I give thee the bucklers.[5]

Margaret

Give us the swords; we have bucklers[6] of our own.

Benedick

If you use them, Margaret, you must put in the pikes with a vice,[7] and they are dangerous weapons for maids.°

virgins

Margaret

Well, I will call Beatrice to you, who I think hath legs.[8]

1 *How pitiful I deserve*

Benedick interprets the line as "How pitifully undeserving I am," though it should be "How much I deserve pity." Benedick sings a popular song that presents the complaint of an unrequited lover who hopes for the favors of the lady. In the New Cambridge edition of the play (2003), F. H. Mares supplies a full text of the song, composed by William Elderton and first appearing in print in 1562. On other songs in the play see note to 2.3.61.

2 *Leander*

A figure from classical myth; Leander was the lover of Hero, and nightly swam across the Hellespont to see her until he drowned in a terrible storm.

3 *Troilus*

Troilus, a Trojan prince, and Cressida carried on their love affair with the help of Cressida's uncle Pandarus. Cressida eventually ended up with a Greek warrior, bartered for a captured Trojan soldier.

4 *quondam carpetmongers*

Former (*quondam*) knights who now avoid fighting and spend their time courting women in their carpeted chambers

5 *turned over and over*

I.e., head over heels

6 *hard*

Harsh; ill-fitting because "horn" and "scorn" recall cuckoldry

7 *under a rhyming planet*

i.e., under an astrological sign that disposes me to write poetry

8 *in festival terms*

With fancy words

Benedick

And therefore will come.

[*sings*] The god of love
That sits above,
And knows me, and knows me,
How pitiful I deserve—[1]

I mean in singing. But in loving, Leander[2] the good swimmer, Troilus[3] the first employer of panders,° and a whole bookful of these quondam carpetmongers,[4] whose names yet run smoothly in the even° road of a blank verse, why, they were never so truly turned over and over[5] as my poor self in love. Marry, I cannot show it in rhyme. I have tried. I can find out no rhyme to "lady" but "baby"—an innocent rhyme; for "scorn," "horn" —a hard[6] rhyme; for "school," "fool"—a babbling rhyme; very ominous endings. No, I was not born under a rhyming planet,[7] nor I cannot woo in festival terms.[8]

go-betweens

uniform; smooth

Enter **Beatrice**.

Sweet Beatrice, wouldst thou come when I called thee?

Beatrice

Yea, signior, and depart when you bid me.

Benedick

Oh, stay but till then!

Beatrice

"Then" is spoken. Fare you well now. And yet, ere I go, let me go with that° I came,° which is, with knowing what hath passed between you and Claudio.

that which / came for

Benedick

Only foul words, and thereupon I will kiss thee.

1 *If you spite it for my sake, I will spite it for yours, for I will never love that which my friend hates.*

I.e., if you are only able to love me by rejecting the natural inclinations of your heart, then I will reject your heart too, since I could never embrace what my lover rejects. Beatrice's convoluted way of saying that she will not love Benedick unless he loves her unreservedly is a sign of her emotional defensiveness.

2 *It appears not in this confession: there's not one wise man among twenty that will praise himself.*

Your wisdom is not apparent in your statement: wise men do not praise themselves.

3 *in the time of good neighbors*

In the days when neighbors were generous with compliments

4 *bell*

I.e., the church bell that tolls for a death

Beatrice

offensive

Foul words is but foul wind, and foul wind is but foul breath, and foul breath is noisome.° Therefore I will depart unkissed.

Benedick

frightened / its — *has received* — *proclaim* — *attributes*

Thou hast frighted° the word out of his° right sense, so forcible is thy wit. But I must tell thee plainly, Claudio undergoes° my challenge, and either I must shortly hear from him or I will subscribe° him a coward. And, I pray thee, now tell me for which of my bad parts° didst thou first fall in love with me?

Beatrice

well governed — *experience*

For them all together, which maintained so politic° a state of evil that they will not admit any good part to intermingle with them. But for which of my good parts did you first suffer° love for me?

Benedick

expression

"Suffer love"! A good epithet!° I do "suffer love" indeed, for I love thee against my will.

Beatrice

In spite of your heart, I think. Alas, poor heart! If you spite it for my sake, I will spite it for yours, for I will never love that which my friend hates.[1]

Benedick

Thou and I are too wise to woo peaceably.

Beatrice

It appears not in this confession: there's not one wise man among twenty that will praise himself.[2]

Benedick

saying — *remembrance*

An old, an old instance,° Beatrice, that lived in the time of good neighbors.[3] If a man do not erect in this age his own tomb ere he dies, he shall live no longer in monument° than the bell[4] rings and the widow weeps.

1 *Question*

I.e., an easy question

2 *Don Worm*

The conscience was proverbially figured as a worm or serpent gnawing at the soul.

3 *old coil*

I.e., a tremendous uproar

Beatrice

And how long is that, think you?

Benedick

ringing *i.e., weeping* *herald; proclaimer*

Question:[1] why, an hour in clamor° and a quarter in rheum.° Therefore is it most expedient for the wise, if Don Worm,[2] his conscience, find no impediment to the contrary, to be the trumpet° of his own virtues, as I am to myself. So much for praising myself, who, I myself will bear witness, is praiseworthy. And now tell me, how doth your cousin?

Beatrice

Very ill.

Benedick

And how do you?

Beatrice

Very ill, too.

Benedick

feel better

Serve God, love me, and mend.° There will I leave you too, for here comes one in haste.

Enter **Ursula**.

Ursula

deceived *right now*

Madam, you must come to your uncle. Yonder's old coil[3] at home. It is proved my lady Hero hath been falsely accused, the Prince and Claudio mightily abused,° and Don John is the author of all, who is fled and gone. Will you come presently?°

Beatrice

Will you go hear this news, signior?

1 *die in thy lap*

Benedick commits himself to a lifetime with Beatrice and sexualizes it, punning on the common Elizabethan slang usage of *die* to mean "reach orgasm."

Benedick

I will live in thy heart, die in thy lap,[1] and be buried in thy eyes—and, moreover, I will go with thee to thy uncle's. [*They*] *exit.*

1 **Act 5, Scene 3**

This scene was omitted in most productions from David Garrick's (1748–1766) to those of the late 19th century. Solemn, ritualistic, and musical, it can be a moving demonstration of Claudio's penitence and a transition between the fractured nuptial and the concluding festivity. Claudio and others process to Leonato's monument. Claudio (or a lord, as the Quarto has it—possibly yet another proxy) reads and hangs up a scroll on a movable property or stage column; the scroll may or may not remain on stage for the reunion scene. Claudio or Balthasar sings a song; Claudio or a lord vows to do an annual rite of penance. In this scene Claudio perhaps fulfills Antonio's request to hang an epitaph on Hero's tomb and *sing it to her bones* (5.1.278), though everything depends on the role one assigns to him in the scene. See *Much Ado About Nothing* on the Early Modern Stage; Alan C. Dessen, *Recovering Shakespeare's Theatrical Vocabulary* (Cambridge: Cambridge Univ. Press, 1995), 34–38.

2 tapers

Candles

3 (song)

It is not clear who is meant to sing this, as the Quarto does not indicate a singer although Claudio clearly requests the song to be sung. This edition assigns it to the Musicians since it seems (*our; us*) to presume multiple voices. The invocation to Diana, *goddess of the night* (line 12) and chastity, protector of virgins, recalls Claudio's earlier reference to Hero, who seemed as chaste *as Dian in her orb* (4.1.55). Immediately before the song, the epitaph celebrates eternal life in fame not in Heaven, and immediately after there is mention of Roman deities *Phoebus* (line 26), god of the sun, and *Hymen* (line 32), god of marriage. The call to *Midnight* (line 16) and the circling around the tomb while singing (clockwise, presumably, the traditional way to ward off evil) all suggest an occult ritual. The command to the graves to yield their dead *Till death be utterèd* (line 20) may mean (1) until the grief has been fully expressed; (2) until death is finally vanquished. Shakespeare clearly characterizes the song and the entire ritual as pagan not Christian, perhaps to avoid the impropriety of staging anything like a church service for one who is not really dead.

4 *goddess of the night*

I.e., Diana, goddess of the moon and chastity

Act 5, Scene 3[1]

Enter **Claudio**, [**Don Pedro**], *and three or four* [**Lords**] *with tapers,*[2] [*and* **Musicians**].

Claudio

Is this the monument of Leonato?

First Lord

It is, my lord.

Claudio

[*reading*] "Done to death by slanderous tongues
Was the Hero that here lies.
recompense Death, in guerdon° of her wrongs,
Gives her fame which never dies;
from So the life that died with° shame
Lives in death with glorious fame."
[*hangs the scroll*] Hang thou there upon the tomb,
Praising her when I am dumb.
Now, music, sound, and sing your solemn hymn.

Musicians

(*song*)[3] Pardon, goddess of the night,[4]
i.e., Hero Those that slew thy virgin knight,°
For the which with songs of woe
Round about her tomb they go.
Midnight, assist our moan.
Help us to sigh and groan
Heavily, heavily.
Graves, yawn and yield your dead,
Till death be utterèd,
Heavily, heavily.

Claudio

Now, unto thy bones good night!
Yearly will I do this rite.

1 *wheels of Phoebus*

The sun god's chariot, which drew the sun across the sky

2 *Each his several way.*

All of you go your separate ways.

3 *Hymen now with luckier issue speed's*

Let Hymen, god of marriage, send us a happier outcome.

Don Pedro

morning Good morrow,° masters. Put your torches out.
finished hunting The wolves have preyed,° and look, the gentle day,
Before the wheels of Phoebus,[1] round about
Dapples the drowsy east with spots of grey.
Thanks to you all, and leave us. Fare you well.

Claudio

Good morrow, masters. Each his several way.[2]

[**Lords** *and* **Musicians** *exit.*]

Don Pedro

clothes Come, let us hence and put on other weeds,°
And then to Leonato's we will go.

Claudio

And Hymen now with luckier issue speed 's[3]
this woman Than this° for whom we rendered up this woe.

They exit.

1 *some fault*

Borachio says that Margaret *knew not what she did when she spoke to me* (5.1.294), so the *fault* must be merely that of dressing in Hero's clothes, allowing, if innocently, the deception.

2 *against her will*

I.e., unintentionally

Act 5, Scene 4

Enter **Leonato**, [**Antonio**,] **Benedick**, [**Beatrice**,] **Margaret**, **Ursula**, **Friar** [**Francis**], *and* **Hero**.

Friar Francis

Did I not tell you she was innocent?

Leonato

So are the Prince and Claudio, who accused her
On the basis of Upon° the error that you heard debated.
But Margaret was in some fault[1] for this,
Although against her will,[2] as it appears
investigation In the true course of all the question.°

Antonio

work out Well, I am glad that all things sorts° so well.

Benedick

otherwise / my promise And so am I, being else° by faith° enforced
i.e., duel To call young Claudio to a reckoning° for it.

Leonato

Well, daughter, and you gentlewomen all,
Withdraw into a chamber by yourselves,
And when I send for you, come hither masked.
The Prince and Claudio promised by this hour
duty To visit me.—You know your office,° brother.
You must be father to your brother's daughter,
And give her to young Claudio. *Ladies exit.*

Antonio

serious Which I will do with confirmed° countenance.

Benedick

help Friar, I must entreat your pains,° I think.

Friar Francis

To do what, signior?

1 *bind me or undo me*

Tie the marriage knot or ruin (punning on *undo* as "untie") me

2 *eye of favor*

Favorable eye, i.e., positively

3 *requite her*

Return her love

Benedick

To bind me or undo me[1]—one of them.
—Signior Leonato, truth it is, good signior,
Your niece regards me with an eye of favor.[2]

Leonato

That eye my daughter lent her? 'Tis most true.

Benedick

And I do with an eye of love requite her.[3]

Leonato

The sight whereof I think you had from me,
From Claudio, and the Prince. But what's your will?

Benedick

Your answer, sir, is enigmatical.
as for / is that But for° my will, my will is° your good will
May stand with ours, this day to be conjoined
In the state of honorable marriage
—In which, good Friar, I shall desire your help.

Leonato

My heart is with your liking.

Friar Francis

And my help.
Here comes the Prince and Claudio.

Enter [**Don Pedro**] *and* **Claudio**, *and two or three other.*

Don Pedro

Good morrow to this fair assembly.

Leonato

Good morrow, Prince. Good morrow, Claudio.
still We here attend you. Are you yet° determined
Today to marry with my brother's daughter?

1 *Ethiope*

Dark skinned (conventionally taken as unattractive) person

2 *savage bull*

The joke is that Benedick is about to "bear the yoke" (as he himself swore he would never do in 1.1.229–234), but the reference is extended in lines 46–49; see note 3 below.

3 *Europa did at lusty Jove / When he would play the noble beast in love*

In classical mythology, Jove, in the form of a white bull, seduced the Phoenician princess Europa, one of his many mortal lovers.

4 *had an amiable low*

Made seductive sounds (*low* is the sound made by a cow or a bull)

5 *got a calf*

Fathered a calf (with a play on *calf* meaning "simpleton")

6 *reck'nings*

Matters to settle

7 *seize upon*

Take possession of

Claudio

commitment I'll hold my mind° were she an Ethiope.[1]

Leonato

Call her forth, brother. Here's the Friar ready.

[**Antonio** *exits.*]

Don Pedro

Good morrow, Benedick. Why, what's the matter
i.e., forbidding That you have such a February° face,
So full of frost, of storm, and cloudiness?

Claudio

I think he thinks upon the savage bull.[2]
paint —Tush, fear not, man. We'll tip° thy horns with gold,
Europe And all Europa° shall rejoice at thee,
As once Europa did at lusty Jove
When he would play the noble beast in love.[3]

Benedick

Bull Jove, sir, had an amiable low,[4]
mounted And some such strange bull leapt° your father's cow
And got a calf[5] in that same noble feat
Much like to you, for you have just his bleat.

Claudio

this insult For this° I owe you. Here comes other reck'nings.[6]

Enter [**Antonio**], **Hero**, **Beatrice**, **Margaret**, **Ursula**, [*the ladies all wearing masks*].

Which is the lady I must seize upon?[7]

Leonato

This same is she, and I do give you her.

Claudio

Why, then she's mine.—Sweet, let me see your face.

1 *like of me*

Like me; are pleased by me

2 *Soft and fair*

Wait a moment (polite)

Leonato

No. That you shall not till you take her hand
Before this Friar and swear to marry her.

Claudio

[*to* **Hero**] Give me your hand before this holy Friar.
I am your husband, if you like of me.[1]

[*He takes her hand.*]

Hero

[*unmasking*] And when I lived, I was your other wife,
And when you loved, you were my other husband.

Claudio

Another Hero!

Hero

Nothing certainer.
slandered One Hero died defiled,° but I do live,
And surely as I live, I am a maid.

Don Pedro

The former Hero! Hero that is dead!

Leonato

merely She died, my lord, but° whiles her slander lived.

Friar Francis

explain; moderate All this amazement can I qualify,°
When, after that the holy rites are ended,
in full I'll tell you largely° of fair Hero's death.
these marvels / normal Meantime, let wonder° seem familiar,°
(go) immediately And to the chapel let us presently.°

Benedick

Soft and fair,[2] Friar.—Which is Beatrice?

Beatrice

[*unmasking*] I answer to that name. What is your will?

Benedick

Do not you love me?

1 *'Tis no such matter.*

It is nothing of the sort.

2 *in friendly recompense*

Only as a friend

3 *of his own pure brain*

All of his own making

Beatrice

Why no, no more than reason.

Benedick

Why, then your uncle and the Prince and Claudio
Have been deceived. They swore you did.

Beatrice

Do not you love me?

Benedick

In truth Troth° no, no more than reason.

Beatrice

Why, then my cousin, Margaret, and Ursula
Are much deceived, for they did swear you did.

Benedick

They swore that you were almost sick for me.

Beatrice

They swore that you were well-nigh dead for me.

Benedick

'Tis no such matter.[1] Then you do not love me?

Beatrice

No, truly, but in friendly recompense.[2]

Leonato

Come, cousin, I am sure you love the gentleman.

Claudio

And I'll be sworn upon 't that he loves her,
handwriting For here's a paper written in his hand, °
rhythmically awkward A halting° sonnet of his own pure brain [3]
Addressed Fashioned° to Beatrice. [*shows paper*]

Hero

And here's another,
Writ in my cousin's hand, stol'n from her pocket,
Containing her affection unto Benedick. [*shows paper*]

1 *our own hands against our hearts*

Our own hands have testified against our hearts (but possibly also: "our own hands are pressed against our hearts").

2 *in a consumption*

Wasting away from illness

3 **Leonato**

Reading the line as a stage direction for a kiss (cf. Beatrice, earlier, *stop his mouth with a kiss*, 2.1.278–279), editors generally substitute Benedick for Leonato here, against the evidence of both the Quarto and Folio. But Leonato could easily speak the line in his role as master of the ceremonies and new harmonies, bringing an end to the lovers' foolish wrangling by directing them to an embrace. See Alan C. Dessen, *Rescripting Shakespeare* (Cambridge: Cambridge Univ. Press, 2002), 214–215.

4 *If a man will be beaten with brains, 'a shall wear nothing handsome about him.*

If a man fears being mocked, he will not even risk dressing fashionably.

5 *double-dealer*

(1) married man; one who is no longer single; (2) adulterer

6 *look exceedingly narrowly to thee*

Watch you very closely

Benedick

A miracle! Here's our own hands against our hearts.[1] Come, I will have thee, but, by this light, I take thee for pity.

Beatrice

I would not deny you, but, by this good day, I yield upon great persuasion, and partly to save your life, for I was told you were in a consumption.[2]

Leonato[3]

Peace! I will stop your mouth.

[**Beatrice** *and* **Benedick** *kiss.*]

Don Pedro

How dost thou, Benedick the married man?

Benedick

assembly / jesters I'll tell thee what, Prince: a college° of wit-crackers°
mock / mood cannot flout° me out of my humor.° Dost thou think
I care for a satire or an epigram? No. If a man will be
he beaten with brains, 'a° shall wear nothing handsome
intend about him.[4] In brief, since I do purpose° to marry, I
will think nothing to any purpose that the world can
say against it, and therefore never flout at me for what
I have said against it, for man is a giddy thing, and this
is my conclusion.—For thy part, Claudio, I did think
to have beaten thee, but in that thou art
likely like° to be my kinsman, live unbruised and love my
cousin.

Claudio

I had well hoped thou wouldst have denied Beatrice,
so that that° I might have cudgeled thee out of thy single life
to make thee a double-dealer,[5] which, out of question, thou wilt be if my cousin do not look exceedingly narrowly to thee.[6]

1 *wives' heels*

I.e., as they dance; but a further joke about female sexuality, though here within the sanction of marriage. Compare 3.4.42 and note.

2 *horn*

Benedick can't resist a last reference to cuckold's horns.

Benedick

Come, come, we are friends. Let's have a dance ere we are married, that we may lighten our own hearts and our wives' heels.[1]

Leonato

We'll have dancing afterward.

Benedick

by First, of° my word! Therefore play, music.—Prince, thou art sad. Get thee a wife; get thee a wife. There is *respected; revered* no staff more reverend° than one tipped with horn.[2]

Enter **Messenger**.

Messenger

taken [*to* **Don Pedro**] My lord, your brother John is ta'en° in flight
And brought with armèd men back to Messina.

Benedick

[*to* **Don Pedro**] Think not on him till tomorrow. I'll *worthy* devise thee brave° punishments for him.—Strike up, pipers. [*Music; they*] *dance* [*, and they exit*].

Longer Notes

PAGE 79

1.3.10-11 *I cannot hide what I am*

The great 18th-century editor and critic Samuel Johnson commented: "This is one of our author's natural touches. An envious and unsocial mind, too proud to give pleasure, and too sullen to receive it, always endeavours to hide its malignity from the world and from itself under the plainness of simple honesty, or the dignity of haughty independence" (*The Plays of William Shakespeare*, 8 vols., London, 1765, 3: 186). To create this "envious and unsocial" mind Shakespeare departed from his sources, wherein disappointment in love motivates the plotting. Witness Bandello's Girondo (Don John), hearing news of Fenicia's (Hero's) engagement to Timbreo (Claudio): "This man, hearing the news, was seized with sorrow, for he had just previously fallen in love with Fenicia's beauty, and so fiercely did the flames of love consume his breast that he thought he would surely die if he could not have Fenicia as his wife" (ed. Bullough in For Further Reading).

PAGE 85

2.1.0 *Antonio*

The stage direction in the Quarto identifies Antonio here only as Leonato's "brother," and other speech prefixes and stage directions identify him as "brother" and say he is "old." Since Leonato calls him *Brother Anthony* in 5.1.92, the brother has usually (and sensibly) been identified with the aged and masked Signior Antonio who dances with Ursula in 2.1. This sort of multiple designation appears frequently in playbooks of the period and in this play: in the Quarto Don Pedro is called *Don Peter* (1.1.8) and *the Prince* (2.1.186SD); Don John, *John the Bastard* (1.1.81SD), *Sir John the Bastard* (1.3.0SD), *dumb* [an error for Don] *John* (2.1.72SD), and *Bastard* (3.2.69SP); Dogberry, *the Constable* (3.5.0SD), *Keeper* (4.2.1SP), *Andrew* (for "merry Andrew," i.e., the clown, 4.2.4SP), and frequently throughout one scene in speech prefixes (4.2) *Kemp*, this last referring to Will Kemp, the famous comedian who first played the part. Like all modern editions, this one standardizes character identifications in speech prefixes and stage directions.

PAGE 119

2.2.12–13 *Margaret, the waiting gentlewoman to Hero*

Margaret has a problematic role in Borachio's scheme and in the play. See Leonato's later judgment, *But Margaret was in some fault for this, / Although against her will* (5.4.4–5). There is no precedent for her in Bandello, Shakespeare's source, but there is some in similar stories Shakespeare might have known; in Ariosto's *Orlando Furioso* and Edmund Spenser's *The Faerie Queene* (Bk. 2), for example, a maidservant impersonates her mistress during an assignation. In Shakespeare's play Margaret flirts harmlessly with Benedick during the masquerade (2.1), assists in the deception of Beatrice by running to get her (3.1), jests about the wedding night with Hero and matches Beatrice in repartee (3.4), teases Benedick again (5.2), and appears onstage for final resolution (5.4). No reason is given for her improbable assent to Borachio's odd request to impersonate her mistress while he enters the chamber window by the name of Claudio for a rendezvous (2.2.35–44). And if Margaret is present in 4.1 for the wedding scene, as is likely though she does not appear by name in the stage directions, then audiences must wonder why she says nothing about the imposture during the accusations. At a Washington DC production in 1992, the director provided an answer by having Don

John silence Margaret by stepping in front of her and revealing a dagger (see Cox in the For Further Reading section). Margaret in the Branagh film (1993) is simply too stunned and frightened to reveal her unwitting role in the deception. See also McEachern in For Further Reading, who characterizes Margaret as a social climber in a play much concerned with social status (pp. 13–14).

PAGE 229

4.1.285 *Kill Claudio.*

Ranging over the last two centuries, John F. Cox (see the For Further Reading section) has analyzed various stagings of the line: "Helena Faucit spoke her 'Kill Claudio' half appealingly, half commandingly, in a voice earnest, yet startling in its bitterness and force . . . Louisa Nisbett clasped Benedick impulsively about the neck, fell on his shoulder and burst out sobbing . . . Ellen Kean said the words with concentrated indignation . . . Louisa Herbert with fiery spirit . . . Ellen Terry spoke them less fiercely than some, though with swift impulsiveness, turning with sudden eagerness on Benedick . . . As she matured in the roles she delivered the line with 'concentrated energy,' 'like an arrow from a full-drawn bow,' emphasizing the words with 'a gesture like that of a thrusting lance' . . . Fanny Davenport spoke the words intimately, her lips to Benedick's . . . Helena Modjeska's demand was 'quick and passionate' . . . Sybil Thorndike's 'Kill Claudio' 'nearly killed everyone in the house' . . . In Zeffirelli's hot-blooded Sicilian setting the words were instantly plausible . . . Maggie Smith delivering them 'with a savage force that made laughter unthinkable' . . . Joan Plowright spoke them quietly and matter-of-factly . . . Janet Suzman as a quick response, 'with a break in her voice' signifying 'the terrible nature of her request' . . . Judi Dench with cool intensity, the words creating a sudden impact after the stillness of the preceding love declaration . . . After a long pause, Emma Thompson spoke very slowly with deep, deadly intensity."

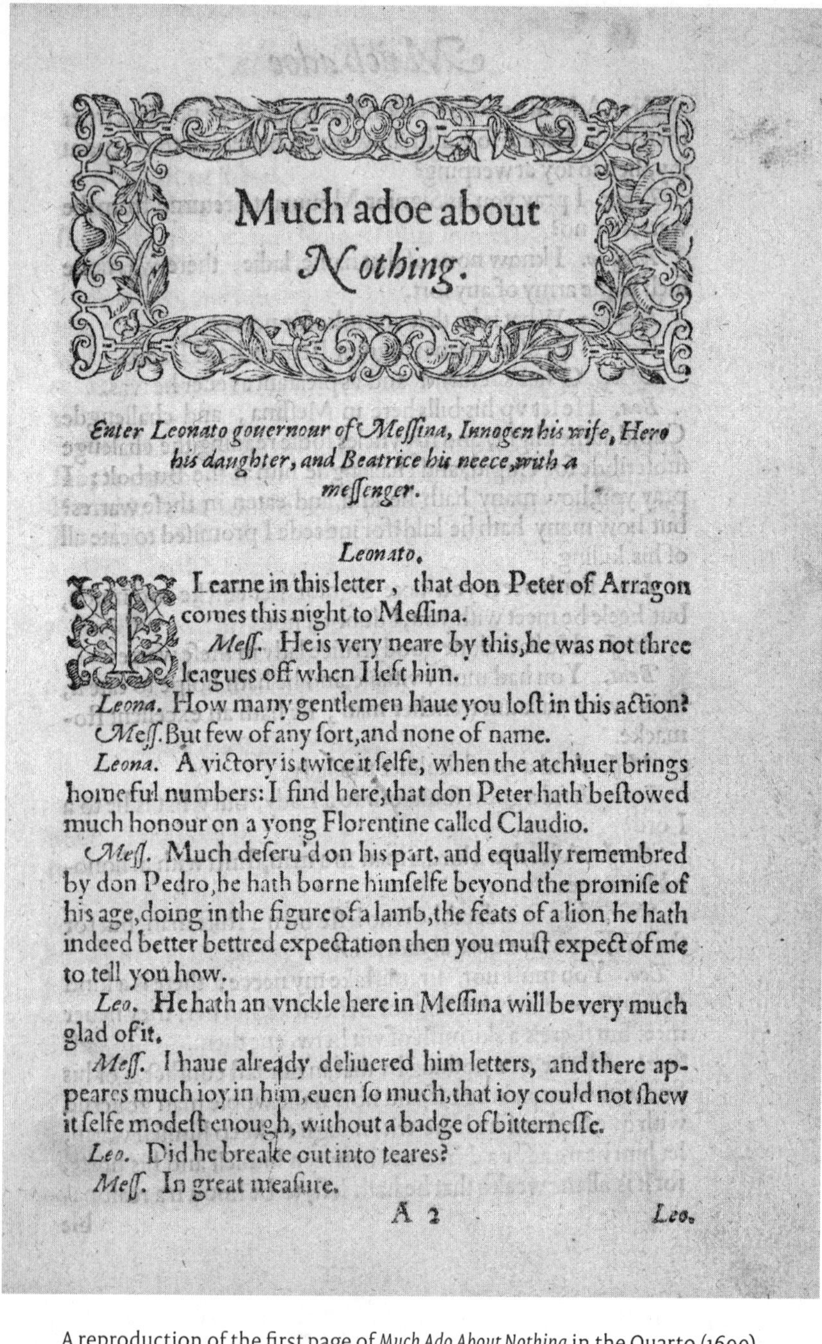

Much adoe about *Nothing.*

Enter Leonato gouernour of Meſſina, Innogen his wife, Hero his daughter, and Beatrice his neece, with a meſſenger.

Leonato.

I Learne in this letter, that don Peter of Arragon comes this night to Meſſina.

Meſſ. He is very neare by this, he was not three leagues off when I left him.

Leona. How many gentlemen haue you loſt in this action?

Meſſ. But few of any ſort, and none of name.

Leona. A victory is twice it ſelfe, when the atchiuer brings home ful numbers: I find here, that don Peter hath beſtowed much honour on a yong Florentine called Claudio.

Meſſ. Much deſeru'd on his part, and equally remembred by don Pedro, he hath borne himſelfe beyond the promiſe of his age, doing in the figure of a lamb, the feats of a lion, he hath indeed better bettred expectation then you muſt expect of me to tell you how.

Leo. He hath an vnckle here in Meſſina will be very much glad of it.

Meſſ. I haue already deliuered him letters, and there appeares much ioy in him, euen ſo much, that ioy could not ſhew it ſelfe modeſt enough, without a badge of bitterneſſe.

Leo. Did he breake out into teares?

Meſſ. In great meaſure.

A 2 *Leo.*

A reproduction of the first page of *Much Ado About Nothing* in the Quarto (1600).

Editing *Much Ado About Nothing*

by David Scott Kastan

M*uch Ado About Nothing* was first printed in 1600 in an inexpensive quarto edition (Q) published by Andrew Wise and William Aspley. The title page states that the play had been "sundry times publicly acted" by Shakespeare's company, the Lord Chamberlain's Men, by the time it appeared in print. It seems likely that the play was ready for performance late in 1598 (sometime after the publication of Frances Meres's *Palladis Tamia* in 1598, which has a list of Shakespeare's comedies but doesn't mention *Much Ado*, and sometime before the comic actor Will Kemp left the company early in 1599, as Kemp, who would have played Dogberry, is named in speech prefixes in Act Four, scene two). The Quarto is generally a well-printed text, but it is not a version of any of the play's "sundry" public performances. It is seemingly derived from a draft, most likely written in Shakespeare's own hand, but one that had not yet worked out all of the specific demands of staging. Stage business is not clearly indicated, a substantial number of necessary exits and entrances are unmarked, characters are inconsistently named in speech prefixes and stage directions, and some characters are named in stage directions (most notably Innogen, Leonato's wife) who never speak and may perhaps remain from an earlier draft but who may have been cut from the revised play. In 1623, the play was reprinted in the Folio, almost certainly from a copy of the Quarto. The Folio text makes a few minor corrections of obvious errors but also introduces some new ones of its own. Thus, this edition is based on the 1600 Quarto, while recognizing that it does not represent Shakespeare's fully worked out theatrical intentions.

In general, the editorial work of this present edition is conservative, accepting the evidence of the printed text rather than hypothesizing what Shakespeare may have written or intended. Most changes from the original merely involve the normalizing of spelling, capitalization, and punctuation; the removal of superfluous italics; the regularization of the names of characters; and the rationalizing of entrances and exits. Emendations are made only when the reading of the Quarto seems manifestly wrong. A comparison of the edited text of 1.1.1–21 with the facsimile page of the Quarto (on p. 304) reveals some of the issues in this process. The speech prefixes are expanded and normalized for clarity, so that *Mess.* and *Leona.* (and *Leo.*) become **Messenger** and **Leonato**. Spelling, capitalization, and italicization in this edition follow modern practices rather than the habits of the Quarto's printers. As neither spelling nor punctuation in Shakespeare's time had yet been standardized, words were spelled in various ways that indicated their proximate pronunciation, and punctuation, which then was largely a rhythmical pointer rather than predominantly designed, as it is now, to clarify logical relations, was necessarily far more idiosyncratic than today. In any case, compositors were under no obligation to follow either the spelling or punctuation of their copy. For most readers, then, there is little advantage in an edition that reproduces the spelling and punctuation of the Quarto text. It does not accurately represent Shakespeare's writing habits, and it makes reading difficult, in a way Shakespeare could never have anticipated or desired.

Therefore "adoe" in the title here becomes the familiar *Ado,* while the title itself is italicized throughout, as is the modern practice. In the first line of the play "Learne" becomes "learn," omitting the intrusive final "e" (and the design capital), just as "neare" in line three of the Quarto gets modernized to "near" and "it selfe" becomes "itself" (though note the long "s" that might be misread as an "f"). In line five "haue" becomes "have" and "atchiuer" in line seven becomes "achiever," though it is interesting to note that "u" was then often used where we use a "v," as "i" could be used where we use a "j," as with the Quarto's "ioy" (for "joy)" two times in line eighteen. In lines one and eight, however, something more than modernization is required: "don Peter" in this edition becomes Don Pedro, capitalizing the honorific as modern practice demands and regularizing the Prince's name as Pedro, which is the form in which it appears in all the rest of the play. Punctuation is modernized throughout. The colon after "numbers" in line eight of the Quarto marks a heavy pause rather than defines a precise grammatical relation as it would in modern usage, and in this text it is replaced with the period that accords with modern practice. Commas that modern usage would not introduce (as that in line one of the Quarto) are omitted, and added when the syntax demands them. In all these cases, editing is intended to clarify rather than alter Shakespeare's intentions. Thus, the Messenger's speech at 1.1.10–14 reads in the Quarto:

> Much deseru'd on his part, and equally remembred by don Pedro, he hath borne himselfe beyond the promise of his age, doing in the figure of a lamb the feats of a lion he hath indeed bettred expectation then you must expect of me to tell you how.

Modernized this reads:

> Much deserved on his part, and equally remembered by Don Pedro. He hath borne himself beyond the promise of his age, doing in the figure of a lamb the feats of a lion. He hath indeed bettered expectation than you must expect of me to tell you how.

Though modernization undoubtedly clarifies the logic of the speech (especially given the lightness of the Quarto's punctuation), admittedly the process involves some loss. Clarity and consistency is gained at the expense of expressive detail, but normalizing spelling, capitalization, and punctuation allows the text to be read with far greater ease than the original, and essentially as it was intended to be understood. We lose the archaic feel of the text in exchange for clarity of meaning. Old spellings are consistently modernized in this edition, but old *forms* of words (e.g., "hath" in the second sentence) are retained. Punctuation, too, is consistently adjusted to reflect modern practice, so punctuation, which was then largely rhythmical in its functioning, here articulates logical relations as it does in modern practice. If, inevitably, in such modernization we lose the historical feel of the text Shakespeare's contemporaries read, it is important to remember that Shakespeare's contemporaries would not have thought the book they read in any sense archaic or quaint, as these details inevitably make it for a reader today. The text would have seemed to them as modern as this one does to us.

Modern readers, however, cannot help but be distracted by the different conventions they encounter on the Quarto page. While it is indeed of interest to see how orthography and typography have changed over time, these changes are not primary concerns for most readers of this edition. What little, then, is lost in a careful modernization of the text is more than made up for by the removal of the artificial obstacle of unfamiliar spelling forms and punctuation habits, which Shakespeare or his publishers never could have intended as interpretive difficulties for his readers.

Textual Notes

The following list records all substantive departures in this edition from the Quarto text of 1600 (Q). It does not usually record modernizations of spelling, normalization in the use of capitals, corrections of obvious typographical errors, adjustments of lineation, minor repositioning or rewording of stage directions (SD), or rationalizations of speech prefixes (SP). Act and scene designations, all absent from the Quarto, also are not recorded. The adopted reading in this edition is given first in boldface and followed by the original, rejected reading of Q1, or noted as being absent from the Quarto text. Editorial stage directions are not collated but are enclosed within brackets in the text. Latin stage directions are translated (e.g., *They all exit* for *Exeunt omnes*).

1.1.1, 8 Pedro Peter; **1.1.36 bird-bolt** Butbolt; **1.1.42 victual** vittaile; **1.1.124 i' God's** a Gods; **1.1.177SD** [in Q entrance includes Iohn the bastard]; **1.1.231 vilely** vildly; **1.1.278 salved** salude; **1.2.0SD Enter Leonato and Antonio** Enter Leonato and an old man brother to Leonato; **1.2.3SP Antonio** Old [and throughout]; **1.2.24 skill** shill; **1.3.47 on** one; **1.3.62 o' my** a my

2.1.0SD [in Q entrance includes a kinsman]; **2.1.10SP, 18SP, 43SP Antonio** brother; **2.1.34 bearherd** Berrord; **2.1.45 curtsy** cursie; **2.1.73SD Enter [Don] Pedro, Claudio, Benedick, Balthasar, [Don] John, [Borachio, Margaret, Ursula, and others, masked. Music plays].** Enter Prince, Pedor Claudio, and Benedick, and Balthasar, or dumb Iohn.; **2.1.73** a bout about; **2.1.186 Enter [Don Pedro,] Hero, and Leonato** Enter the Prince, Hero, Leonato, Iohn and Borachio, and Conrade.; **2.1.298 out o'** out a; **2.3.40 pennyworth** [In Q, this is followed by SD: *Enter Balthaser with musicke*].; **2.3.59 alls done.** [In Q, this is followed by *The Song*. centered on its own line.]; **2.3.72–75 but let . . . nonny** &c.; **2.3.81 lief** liue; **2.3.132 us of** [F] of us; **2.3.237 knife's** kniues

3.1.42 wrestle wrastle; **3.1.63 antic** antique; **3.1.65 vilely** vildly; **3.2.26 can** cannot; **3.2.37 o'** a; **3.2.48SP Don Pedro** Bene.; **3.2.70SP Don John** Bastard. [and throughout scene]; **3.2.71 e'en** den; **3.3.15SP,**

25SP Seacole Watch 2; **3.3.35SP, 42SP, 46SP First Watchman** Watch; **3.3.51SP, 62SP, 81SP, 88SP, 98SP, 114SP Seacole** Watch; **3.3.99 Don** Dun; **3.3.135 vilely** vildly; **3.3.151SP, 157SP Seacole** Watch 2; **3.3.160SP Seacole** [not in Q]; **3.4.17 in** it; **3.4.18 o'** a; **3.4.30 An** &; **3.4.40 o'** a; **3.5.8 off** of; **3.5.21 an** and't

4.1.65SP, 109SP Don John Bastard; **4.1.141–143 Sir, sir, . . . say.** [printed as prose in Q]; **4.1.153–156 Hear me . . . marked** [printed as prose in Q]; **4.1.165 tenor** tenure; **4.1.200 Princes left** princess (left); **4.2.0SD Sexton** Towne clearke; **4.2.1SP Dogberry** Keeper; **4.2.2SP, 5SP Verges** Cowley ; **4.2.4SP Dogberry** Andrew; **4.2.8SP Dogberry** Kemp [and substantively through line 51]; **4.2.16SP Conrade and Borachio** Both; **4.2.44SP Second Watchman** Watch 2; **4.2.46SP Verges** Const.; **4.2.46 the** [not in Q]; **4.2.53SP First Watchman** Watch; **4.2.61SP Dogberry** Constable; **4.2.62SP Verges** Couley; **4.2.63SP Conrade** [not in Q]; **4.2.63 Off** of; **4.2.64SP, 68SP Dogberry** Kemp; **4.2.67SP Conrade** Couley

5.1.1SP Antonio Brother [and throughout scene]; **5.1.16 Bid** And; **5.1.46 e'en (2x)** den; **5.1.165 there's two** theirs two; **5.1.249SP Verges** Con. 2; **5.1.321–322 Bring you . . . lewd fellow** [printed as prose in Q]; **5.2.20–23 The god . . . I deserve** [printed as prose in Q]; **5.3.2SP First Lord** Lord; **5.3.3SP Claudio** [before line eleven in Q]; **5.3.3SD [reading]** [not in Q, which has, centered, *Epitaph.*]; **5.3.12SP Musicians** Song; **5.3.16–17 moan. / Help** mone, help; **5.3.22SP Claudio** Lo.; **5.3.22–23 night! / Yearly** night, yeerely; **5.4.0SD Antonio** old man; **5.4.7SP, 17SP Antonio** Old; **5.4.40 Benedick** Bened.; **5.4.52SD Antonio** brother; **5.4.76–77 Why . . . did** [printed as prose in Q]; **5.4.124 reverend** reverent

Much Ado About Nothing on the Early Stage

by Robert S. Miola

The 1600 Quarto of *Much Ado About Nothing* advertises the play as having been "sundry times publicly acted" by the Lord Chamberlain's Men. At the time of *Much Ado* (1598–1599) this group of actors played under the patronage of Lord Chamberlain George Carey, 2nd Lord Hunsdon. *Much Ado* probably opened at the Curtain, the usual public venue of the company at that time. On August 4, 1600 four plays, including *Much Ado*, were entered in the Stationers' Register (the official list for the publication of plays), "to be staied," i.e., not to be published without further permission. Since three of these four plays (*Much Ado*, *Every Man In His Humor*, and *Henry V*) opened in 1598–1599 and here accompany one new play (*As You Like It*, 1599–1600), Roslyn Landers Knutson plausibly infers that all four were recently in production and that *Much Ado* had moved to the Globe, newly opened in 1599. The play seems to have stayed in repertory; it played twice among other entertainments at court in 1612–1613 for the marriage of James I's daughter Elizabeth to Prince Frederick of Bohemia. Probably present at this performance, the future Charles I later wrote "Benedick and Beatrice" in the Table of Contents of the 1632 Folio, a testimony to the stage presence of those two merry lovers. In the eulogy provided for a 1640 edition of Shakespeare's *Poems* Leonard Digges also attested

Fig 1. In the large London playhouses, the balcony above the stage could be used for staging, seating, or to house musicians.

Fig 2. English Renaissance drama made minimal use of sets or backdrops. In the absence of a set, the stage pillars could be incorporated into the action, standing in for trees and other architectural elements.

Fig 3. The discovery space, located in the middle of the backstage wall, could be used as a third entrance as well as a location for scenes requiring special staging, such as in a tomb or bedchamber.

Fig 4. A trapdoor led to the area below the stage, known as "Hell" (as contrasted with the painted ceiling, known as "Heaven" or the "heavens"). Ghosts or other supernatural figures could descend through the trap, and it could also serve as a grave.

to the drawing power of this couple: "let but Beatrice / And Benedick be seen, lo, in a trice / The cockpit, galleries, boxes, all are full."

What was *Much Ado About Nothing* like on the early modern stage? Fast, for one thing. Elizabethan actors, the evidence suggests, spoke more rapidly than modern ones, delivering the approximately 2,485 lines in two, rather than three, hours. This means that the exchanges between Beatrice and Benedick played like rapid-fire volleys rather than leisurely exchanges of drawing-room wit. Original audiences probably paid little attention to the minute particulars of Don John's plot (and their many improbabilities) but perceived him as a generally threatening, discordant presence: "How tartly that gentleman looks!" says Beatrice; "I never can see him but I am heartburned an hour after" (2.1.3–4).

The rapid delivery of lines perfectly suited the practice of continuous staging, uninterrupted by formal scene divisions or scene changes. This style of staging made meaningful the sequence and juxtaposition of characters and scenes. Beatrice's merry mockery of Don John in Act Two, scene one, immediately followed his sour exit in Act One, scene three, for example, thus defusing the potential seriousness of his malice. Three deceptions appeared in quick succession: Act Two, scene three, the gulling of Benedick; Act Three, scene one, the gulling of Beatrice; and Act Three, scene two, the gulling of Claudio and Don Pedro. The first two are the comic practices of the good Don Pedro; the third is the tragic practice of his half brother Don John. The modern custom of inserting an intermission after Act Three, scene one, or Act Three, scene two, disrupts the sequence and obscures the parallels between the plotting half brothers. The dark gulling in Act Three, scene two, moreover, sharply contrasted with the brightly bumbling comedy of the following Act Three, scene three, wherein Dogberry and company appear as the agents who will apprehend the villains and bring the evil to light. The climactic wedding scene (4.1) shortly after, wherein Claudio cruelly rejects Hero and Beatrice demands his blood, originally played as the central panel of a triptych. The preceding and following scenes featured Dogberry inefficiently and malapropistically laboring to expose the malefactors. The comic frame literally and figuratively contained the tragic action, as the wheels of justice in Messina kept grinding noisily, even if slowly.

The absence of a proscenium arch and scene changes, along with the use of unlocalized settings, centered attention on the large open playing space of the thrust stage. This play brilliantly deployed the space for the *noting* (eavesdropping and perceiving) that appears homonymically in the title *Much Ado About Nothing* (pronounced "not-ing") and throughout the action. In the successive eavesdropping scenes (2.3, 3.1) Benedick and Beatrice probably stationed themselves behind one of the pillars holding up a roof over the stage while their friends played their tricks. Alternatively, some portable covered trellis like the one depicted in the 1615 edition of Thomas Kyd's *The Spanish Tragedy* may have provided the "arbor" (2.3.34) for Benedick's concealment or the "woodbine coverture" (3.1.30) for Beatrice's. The roof over part of the stage served as the "penthouse" (3.3.95) that Borachio and Conrade ducked under to avoid the drizzle and reveal their plot, unaware of the astonished watchmen nearby, overhearing everything. The public playing space also supported the ceremonious entrances, ensemble scenes, and spectacles in the play: the arrival of Don Pedro, Claudio, Benedick, Balthasar, and Don John to Leonato and his household (1.1); the masquerade (2.1); the wedding scene (4.1); and the final resolution (5.4). Unencumbered with realistic scenery, the large open playing space heightened the general awareness of illusion and theatricality. The entire action, played dynamically and continuously, must have appeared as the masquerade scene (2.1) writ large, a rapid succession of playful impostures, deceits, confusions, posings, and exposings.

The style of staging also opened up a register for the occasional symbolic scene, in this play the mourning at the monument of

Leonato (5.3). The scene begins with a procession and music, continues through a ceremonious reading of the epitaph and song, and ends with interlocked rhymes in dialogue (abab). This was probably a more moving, poignant scene on the original stage than it is on modern ones, where it often appears as a stiffly ritualistic and oddly formal interlude. This scene also reveals a number of important Elizabethan stage conventions. Since the plays were performed in daylight, the use of "tapers" (5.3.0SD) indicated a night scene, normally indoors. The scene ends with daybreak, as Don Pedro makes clear:

> Good morrow, masters. Put your torches out.
> The wolves have preyed, and look, the gentle day,
> Before the wheels of Phoebus, round about
> Dapples the drowsy east with spots of grey. (5.3.24–27)

Here poetry provides a change of time and mood, ushering the penitents from grief to the light of resolution and reconciliation, though the "torches," as Alan C. Dessen observes, inconsistently suggest an outdoor scene. (A director has a number of choices here.) The discovery space (an alcove, back center stage) may have served as the monument for Hero dead and the place where Claudio discovers her alive in Act Five, scene four.

The mournful song at the monument expresses grief and penance and illustrates the importance of music on the original stage. The Quarto indicates a *Dance* (2.1.135) in the masquerade while the Folio stage directions call for *"a drum"* (TLN 494) and *"Music for the dance"* (TLN 561). See also note to 2.3.61.

The scene at Leonato's monument also features Don Pedro's brusque direction, "Come, let us hence, and put on other weeds" (5.3.30). The change from mourning garments signals the coming resolution and suggests the importance of costume to the original staging. Don John probably wears throughout the traditional black garb of melancholy. Borachio and Conrade discuss the vagaries of fashion (3.3.119–130). Hero asserts her independence in the choice of her rebato (3.4). Margaret remembers the Duchess of Milan's dress, "cloth o' gold, and cuts, and laced with silver, set with pearls, down sleeves, side sleeves, and skirts round underborne with a bluish tinsel" (3.4.18–20). The hapless town officials appear "*in gowns*" (4.2.0.1SD) at the hearing, Dogberry presumably wearing one of his two (80). Benedick wears a sword when he challenges Claudio (5.1).

Beards also function as various and removable symbols: Beatrice exclaims that she could not endure a husband with a beard (2.1.25–26) but says soon after "he that hath no beard is less than a man" (2.1.30–31); Benedick believes Beatrice loves him because the "white-bearded" (2.3.117–118) fellow (Leonato) says so; he shaves his beard when he becomes a lover (3.2.40–42) but as a fighter taunts Claudio as "Lord Lackbeard" (5.1.186–187). Disguises are usually impenetrable on the early modern stage but not always in this play, as Shakespeare flouts the convention for specific effects: the women, unmasked during the masquerade, see clearly through the men's visors. At the end of the play, however, the men cannot see through the veils worn by the women; they must wait for the women to reveal themselves.

As for the original casting of the play, T. J. King has proposed eleven men and four boys for the principal females, Beatrice, Hero, Margaret, and Ursula. The original company had actors play double roles: the man who played Dogberry or Borachio, for example, might also have played the Friar who appears in Act Four, scene one, and Act Five, scene four. Any available company member could have stepped in for the minor roles—the watchmen, messengers, and attendants. As with Helena and Hermia in *A Midsummer Night's Dream*, Rosalind and Celia in *As You Like It*, the parts of Beatrice and Hero call for a taller boy playing against a shorter one (cf. 1.1.149–151, 186–187). The original

Dogberry was William Kemp, a famous clown who also played Bottom and specialized in broad humor and jigs. Kemp danced his way from London to Norwich on a bet (see his *Kemp's Nine Days' Wonder*, 1600), and may have danced a jig after the play. Richard Cowley, a journeyman actor, originally played Verges, and the folio (1623) calls for a musician named Jack Wilson to enter as Balthasar.

Significant Performances

by Robert S. Miola

(Unless otherwise noted, the performances are identified by the principal actors in the roles of Benedick and Beatrice.)

1598–1599 Lord Chamberlain's Men. See "*Much Ado About Nothing* on the Early Stage."

1612–1613 King's Men. Shakespeare's company revived the play for two performances at court in celebration of a royal wedding.

1748–1776 David Garrick (w. Hannah Pritchard 1748–1756). Garrick and Pritchard played *Ado* as a light comedy that centered on a dazzling contest of wits.

1803–1840 Charles Kemble. Continuing the innovations of his brother John Philip Kemble as Benedick (1788–1790), Charles Kemble broadened the character into a gentleman of honor and feeling.

1836–1879 Helena Faucit. Faucit, similarly, created a Beatrice of wit, deep emotion, spirituality, and goodness.

1843, 1851 William Macready. Macready produced the play with elaborate stage settings and design, including an arched and columned banqueting hall and an ornamental Italian garden.

1845–1865 Charles and Ellen Kean. The Keans continued the Victorian emphasis on pictorial setting, cutting about a quarter of the text to accommodate the scene changes; Ellen Kean's Beatrice was spirited but refined.

1882–1895 Henry Irving and Ellen Terry. Cutting low comedy from the text, Irving mounted a production romantic in mood and lavish in setting. Ellen Terry presented the most widely acclaimed Beatrice ever, a merry charmer who radiated warmth but was capable of darker feelings and emotions.

1904 William Poel, dir. (w. Rita Jolivet, Victor Dougall). Poel broke with the sentimental and spectacular productions of the Victorian past by employing continuous action, rapid speech, a lightly modified text, and simple staging.

1949–1959 John Gielgud (w. Peggy Ashcroft 1950, 1955). Gielgud played Benedick as an urbane courtier who matched wits with a keen and quick Beatrice in a richly visual and superbly paced production that included the low comedy of Dogberry and his company.

1965–1967 Franco Zeffirelli, dir. (w. Maggie Smith 1965–1966). Set in a sensual, hot-blooded Sicily of noisy joyous fiesta, this controversial production used Mediterranean codes of honor and vengeance to make sense of the play, freely modernizing the text and mixing in fantasy elements.

1968–1969 Trevor Nunn, dir. (w. Janet Suzman, Alan Howard). This dark production centered on the broken nuptials and explored the sexual tensions underlying the action.

1976–1977 John Barton, dir. (w. Judi Dench, Donald Sinden). Set in imperial India, Barton exposed the callowness and military arrogance of the men; Dench interpreted Beatrice as a woman who had been cheated by Benedick's "false dice" (2.1.250).

1982–1985 Terry Hands, dir. (w. Sinead Cusack, Derek Jacobi). An openly romantic production, this version of the play featured a Beatrice who, like Dench earlier, mistrusted men and was capable of outrage and fury.

1993 Kenneth Branagh and Emma Thompson, Film. Combining actors from the Royal Shakespeare Company and Hollywood, Branagh directed and starred in this sun-drenched joyful version of the play, which succeeds brilliantly as entertainment but which cuts much text and flattens out some complexities. Emma Thompson plays a wonderfully rich and nuanced Beatrice.

Inspired by *Much Ado About Nothing*

Although *Much Ado About Nothing* ends with multiple weddings, the route to the chapel is neither straight nor easy for the couples concerned. But then, in the real world we often find that love is more random, more risky, and ultimately more prized than we ever could have imagined. Shakespeare's clear-eyed examination of the personal and cultural factors that can threaten romantic relationships has drawn an appreciative response ever since Beatrice, Benedick, Claudio, and Hero first took to the London stage in the sixteenth century. Since that time, generations of subsequent artists have been inspired by Shakespeare's depiction of the ways in which mutual attraction and mutual suspicion can strike sparks off one another, like two good rapiers engaged in play.

Stage

In his 1632 romantic comedy *Hyde Park*, James Shirley draws heavily on *Much Ado About Nothing*, transporting the action to the fashionable London of his own day. Shirley's play celebrates the new freedoms of social interaction that urban men and women were beginning to enjoy—a development encouraged by the construction of new public recreational spaces, such as the park that gives the play its title.

The Hero-Claudio characters in *Hyde Park* are the young Julietta and her suitor, Frank Trier. Determined to test Julietta's faithfulness, Trier introduces her to a notorious womanizer, Lord Bonvile, in the park and then observes her closely to detect any signs of sensual weakness. His sweetheart turns the tables on him, however, first by resisting Lord Bonvile's attempts at seduction so articulately that the one-time lothario declares himself converted to her service and then by rejecting Trier himself. Julietta abandons her inept, Shakespearean suitor in favor of the reformed rake who can properly appreciate her finer qualities. The Beatrice and Benedick subplot also reflects this new, modern sensibility. Whereas in Shakespeare's play the witty duelers are brought together by the scheming of their friends and family, *Hyde Park*'s Beatrice figure, Mistress Carol, takes it upon herself to make a match with the young nobleman Fairfield, claiming to know that he is nearly suicidal with lovesickness and that out of pity she intends to return his love, despite her better intentions. *Hyde Park* cautions seventeenth-century men to abandon their archaic forms of jealousy (such as that which leads Shakespeare's Claudio to denounce Hero) and to instead trust in women's ability to value and defend their own virtue.

The next English stage adaptation of *Much Ado About Nothing* is the less dramatically successful *Law Against Lovers* by William Davenant (c. 1661). Davenant's play is a strange amalgamation of two Shakespearean plays, *Much Ado* and *Measure for Measure*. Davenant does away with Hero and Claudio, swapping them out for the young couple from *Measure*, Julietta and Claudio. Beatrice and Benedick remain, however, their names and personalities intact despite a change in circumstance. Davenant's Beatrice is a noblewoman of the duchy of Savoy. When the Duke of Savoy suddenly absents himself on unexplained business, the duchy falls under the government of Angelo, a stern legislator who revives a "law against lovers" that condemns all those who participate in premarital intercourse to death. Beatrice's fury at the plight of her friend Julietta, whose lover Claudio is thrown in jail and threatened with execution, brings her into accord with her one-time adversary, Benedick, who is the brother of Angelo but disagrees with his sibling's policies and actions. Reconciled by politics, and admiring of one another's conduct in the pursuit of justice for the miserable Claudio, Beatrice and Benedick decide to marry once the rightful Duke returns to his dominions, Claudio's sentence is repealed, and peace returns to Savoy.

In William Congreve's *The Way of the World* (c. 1700), sexual intrigue is entirely *à la mode*. Congreve depicts a London in which the new cosmopolitanism depicted by Shirley has devolved into a kind of jaded, adulterous social round. Not only can men and women not trust one another, they cannot even trust their own kind: in one scene, a woman tells her friend that men are not to be trusted, and that "if we will be happy, we must find the means in ourselves, and among ourselves"—not realizing that her friend is secretly having an affair with her husband. Congreve's London is a corrupt society, and his characters have developed their verbal skills in order to navigate it safely and more effectively. Congreve's dueling lovers, Mrs. Millamant and Mr. Mirabell, have fought one another to a détente early on and are, in fact, secretly betrothed at the start of the play. But financial necessity forces them to pretend a less serious involvement until they can figure out how to free Millamant's fortune from the legal control of her guardian, who hates Mirabell intensely. The lovers must therefore deny, avoid, and conceal any hint of their plans to marry. Their acting skill and their witty repartee serves them well in this case; they protest their love in order to shield it from others. In *The Way of the World*, Millamant's true opponent isn't Mirabell. She fears betrayal not from him, but from the treacherous society within which they both must live and that (rather than her witty sparring partner) must be held at bay at all costs.

Congreve's portrait of adulterous London life seems to have struck the following generation of theatergoers as unnecessarily bawdy, and in 1736, James Miller tried to reclaim *Much Ado* and produce a Shakespearean tribute high in moral decency. His adaptation, *The Universal Passion*, returns the action of the play to Italy and makes the Hero-Claudio pair, Bellario and Lucilia, initially more ridiculous and finally more sympathetic than Shakespeare's inexperienced lovers. *Much Ado*'s Claudio doesn't know how to woo Hero, and Hero herself seems to communicate mostly via coy smiles and whispered confirmations. Bellario and Lucilia, however, are even more touchingly inept because they truly believe they know how to proceed. Bellario decides to pique Lucilia's interest using reverse psychology: he proclaims his indifference to her charms, but once she is provoked and begins to pursue him, it is all his counselors can do to keep him from blowing his cover by responding too eagerly. If the beginning of the play is even more lighthearted than that of *Much Ado*, however, Miller treats Bellario's stinging repudiation of Lucilia very seriously. In Miller's version of events, Lucilia never fully regains her trust in Bellario. The newly wary girl does not explicitly agree to her "resurrected" marriage in the play's final act, merely remaining silent as she allows her cousin Liberia (the Beatrice figure) to join her hands with her husband's. *The Universal Passion* attempts to depict innocence in place of Congreve's depraved sophistication, but it also depicts how the acquisition of experience exacts great costs from previously innocent individuals.

Film

Much Ado About Nothing has been successfully filmed several times, and this is perhaps the reason why it has garnered few movie adaptations. However, one could broadly claim that most films about bickering lovers are to some degree indebted to the Beatrice-Benedick model. In his 1981 book *Pursuits of Happiness*, the philosopher Stanley Cavell describes a film genre that he calls "the Hollywood comedy of remarriage." These films, he suggests, inherit "the preoccupations and discoveries of Shakespearean romantic comedy," and therefore it makes sense for us to discuss a few of these movies' family resemblance to *Much Ado.*

Two classic films discussed in Cavell's book offer important (though admittedly limited) plot parallels with the Shakespearean play: Howard Hawks's *His Girl Friday* (1940) and George Cukor's *The Philadelphia Story* (1940). Both films track a divorced couple that meets on the eve of the woman's remarriage, and both emphasize the uneasy emotional fluctuations—encompassing both past intimacy as well as present animosity—that those couples experience. In *Much Ado,* Beatrice suggests that she and Benedick have loved before but that their earlier relationship ended poorly. Their animosity relies on their long association with one another, as they embody the old maxim that familiarity breeds contempt. In *His Girl Friday,* ex-marrieds Walter and Hildy meet on good terms at the office of the newspaper where she used to work and where he is still editor-in-chief, but their affection is tempered by a wariness born of experience. Likewise in *The Philadelphia Story,* heiress Tracy Lord and her ex-husband, C. K. Dexter Haven, meet two years after their divorce and engage in some fond banter. However, this playful feuding is balanced by the film's silent opening sequence, which shows Dexter's final departure: Tracy breaks his golf club over her knee, and he pushes her backward over the threshold of the family home. The intimate knowledge these characters have of their former partners is the cause of their present hostility, but it is also the source of their future hope of reunion. As long as both individuals are willing to admit when the other side has scored a significant point—that is to say, as long as knowledge of one's partner leads to self-knowledge, as well—a thorough awareness, understanding of, and respect for one's partner can successfully repair a fractured union.

A modern, cross-cultural take on *Much Ado About Nothing* can be found in the 2001 Bollywood romantic comedy *Dil Chahta Hai* ("The Heart Desires"), directed by Farhan Akhtar. The movie, which divides its action between India and Australia, focuses on the fortunes of three close friends who have recently graduated from college. Akash, Siddharth, and Sameer are inseparable companions whose friendship sometimes takes a toll on their romantic engagements, just as, in *Much Ado*, the close camaraderie between Don Pedro, Claudio, and Benedick threatens their ability to meet, court, and trust women. *Dil Chahta Hai* follows the trio as they figure out their various philosophies on love and begin to think about the direction their adult lives will take. Akash, the most Benedick-like of the group, resists the idea of a lasting attachment to any one woman. He lives by the rule of the two-week relationship—until, that is, he meets the beautiful Shalini at a nightclub in Mumbai. She initially rebuffs him, but when they meet again in Australia the acquaintance develops into a friendship that allows them jokingly to compare their beliefs about love. Like Beatrice and Benedick, Shalini and Akash construct a relationship that hovers between seriousness and jest, between devotion and indifference, and neither one seems fully aware of what the "heart desires." In the end, just as in *Much Ado*, it will take the counsel and intervention of friends to bring about the admission and resolution of their mutual affection.

In 2005, the BBC brought *Much Ado* into the twenty-first century with an adaptation that transports the romantic Italian antics to a modern English television station. When Wessex Tonight needs a replacement newscaster, station boss Leonard hires the smooth-talking Benedick for the job. Problems arise when it's revealed that Benedick once had an ill-fated affair with the show's co-anchor, Beatrice. The other crewmembers decide to intervene to get Beatrice and Benedick back together. In this BBC telefilm—part of a series of four modern adaptations collectively titled *ShakespeaRe-Told*—Leonard's daughter Hero, the beautiful weathergirl, takes a liking to Claude, the handsome sports reporter. The villain of the newsroom is the lonely editor Don, who carries a torch for Hero and convinces Claude that she's been unfaithful in order to break up the couple on the eve of their wedding. David Nicholls's adaptation is written with modern dialogue occasionally interspersed with Shakespeare's own lines. But the language isn't the only thing that's been modernized in this production. After Claude leaves Hero at the altar, rather than passively suffer her father's accusations, Hero confronts Don and demands to know why he has slandered her. Don pushes Hero, who falls on her head and lands in a coma. A penitent Claude remains by her hospital bedside and is overjoyed when she awakes, though Hero isn't so sure she's ready to forgive him. At the end of this progressive tale, Beatrice and Benedick prepare to wed, while Claude waits to see if the aggrieved Hero will ever take him back.

Dance and Music

The most famous musical adaptation of the play is the French composer Hector Berlioz's comic opera *Béatrice et Bénédict*, first performed in 1862. Berlioz was a great Romantic interpreter of Shakespeare who dealt uniquely with the dilemma all respectful adaptors must face: namely, that while changes must be made in order to create a new work of art, those changes necessarily do violence to the original material. Something new is gained, as something old is lost. By restricting the two-act libretto to the more mature and wittier lovers, Berlioz gives his opera a tighter dramatic focus, making the story conform better to the demands of operatic performance. He loses, however, the tragic Hero-Claudio plotline entirely. At the same time as he makes this cut, though, Berlioz reminds us of this loss—as if encouraging us to reread our own copies of *Much Ado About Nothing*—by making Hero what one critic has called "the most musically developed character" in the entire work.

The classic dance adaptation of *Much Ado* can be found in the repertoire of Moscow's Bolshoi Ballet. Entitled *Love for Love*, the Bolshoi production has a musical score by composer Tikhon

Khrennikov. It was first performed in 1976 and remains a regular, well-loved offering. The librettists, Vera Boccadoro and Boris Pokrovsky, made a number of changes to Shakespeare's plot. In their version of the story, Claudio and Benedick appear as returning Crusaders, whose welcome to Signior Leonato's home sets the scene for peacetime romance between Hero and Claudio and, in a warier and more strenuous way, between Benedick and Beatrice. The villain Don John, whose destructive behavior in Shakespeare's play remains relatively unexplained (and perhaps inexplicable), becomes in the ballet a familiar type of evildoer: a failed suitor whose jealousy of his successful rival, Claudio, leads him to perform acts of mischief.

In 1986, at the China Shakespeare Festival in Shanghai, the Anhui Huangmei Opera Troupe transformed *Much Ado* into a traditional Chinese opera in the *huangmei* style. Characterized by light, lyrical music, *huangmei* opera originated in rural peasant performances, and contemporary *huangmei* performances typically maintain a local, folk art flavor. *Huangmei* opera also emphasizes duets and dancing, making it particularly suitable for romantic stories. Adaptor Jin Zhi set the tale in ancient China and rechristened Shakespeare's characters with Chinese names. To help Chinese audiences overcome the foreignness of the Western tale, Jin Zhi set the opera in a town on the country's far border, which allowed the production to incorporate certain aspects of Chinese culture while also justifying the story's more exotic elements. The masquerade, for example, was mixed with a traditional lantern dance. By making their *Much Ado* a tale explicitly about minority life in ancient China, the Anhui troupe managed to create an adaptation that was both highly novel and eminently familiar to its audiences.

For Further Reading
by Robert S. Miola

Berger, Harry, Jr. "Against the Sink-a-Pace: Sexual and Family Politics in *Much Ado About Nothing.*" *Shakespeare Quarterly*, 33 (1982), 302–313. Berger explores the premises of power and male solidarity in the play.

Branagh, Kenneth, dir. *Much Ado About Nothing.* Samuel Goldwyn Co., 1993. Film. Screenplay, Introduction, and Notes by Branagh. New York: W. W. Norton, 1993. See also Anne Barton's balanced review, "Shakespeare in the Sun." *New York Review of Books*, 27 May 1993, 11–13; Samuel Crowl's analysis of Hollywood antecedents, *Shakespeare at the Cineplex: The Kenneth Branagh Era*. Athens, Ohio: Ohio Univ. Press, 2003. Pp. 64–78.

Bullough, Geoffrey. *Narrative and Dramatic Sources of Shakespeare.* 8 vols. London: Routledge & Kegan Paul, 1957–1975. Vol. 2: 61–139. After a detailed introduction, Bullough reprints a translation of the source story from Bandello's *Novelle*, along with other possible sources and analogues.

Cox, John F., ed. *Much Ado About Nothing. Shakespeare in Production* series. Cambridge: Cambridge Univ. Press, 1997. This edition offers a full stage history of the play and a line-by-line commentary of theatrical interpretation. Also his, "The Stage Representation of the 'Kill Claudio' sequence in *Much Ado About Nothing*," *Shakespeare Survey*, 32 (1979), 27–36.

Everett, Barbara. "*Much Ado About Nothing*: the unsociable comedy." *English Comedy*, ed. Michael Cordner, Peter Holland, and John Kerrigan. Cambridge: Cambridge Univ. Press, 1994. Pp. 68–84. Everett perceptively analyzes the mingling of joy and sorrow in the play.

Jenkins, Harold. "The Ball Scene in *Much Ado About Nothing*." *Shakespeare: Text, Language, Criticism: Essays in Honour of Marvin Spevack*, ed. Bernhard Fabian and Kurt Tetzeli von Rosador. Hildesheim: Olms-Weidmann, 1987. Pp. 98–117. Jenkins gives a clear and searching account of textual, theatrical, and interpretive issues in a pivotal scene of the play.

Leggatt, Alexander. *Shakespeare's Comedy of Love*. London: Methuen, 1974. Pp. 151–183. Leggatt sensitively reviews the play and its relation to other Shakespearean comedies as well as its use of both formalism and naturalism.

Mares, F. H., ed. *Much Ado About Nothing*. Cambridge: Cambridge Univ. Press, (updated) 2003. Mares provides a full introduction and an account of recent theatrical and critical interpretation, along with supplementary notes and appendices on specific problems.

Mason, Pamela. "Don Pedro, Don John, and Don . . . who?—Noting a Stranger in *Much Adoodle do*." *Shakespeare and his Contemporaries in Performance*, ed. Edward J. Esche. Aldershot: Ashgate, 2000. Pp. 241–260. Mason discusses Benedick's character and the misperceptions created by common theatrical cuts and editorial decisions.

McEachern, Claire, ed. *Much Ado About Nothing*. London: Thomson Learning, 2006. This Arden edition provides a full and well-informed discussion of textual, critical, and theatrical issues.

Miola, Robert S. *Shakespeare and Classical Comedy: The Influence of Plautus and Terence*. Oxford: Clarendon Press, 1994. Pp. 79–100. Pairing the play with *Shrew*, a chapter analyzes Shakespeare's adaptation of classical and Italian sources and traditions in the play.

Neely, Carol Thomas. *Broken Nuptials in Shakespeare's Plays*. New Haven: Yale Univ. Press, 1985. Pp. 24–57. This first-generation feminist account explores gender-based fantasies and anxieties about sex and power in the play.

Redmond, Michael J. "'Tis common knowledge': Italian Stereotypes and Audience Response in *Much Ado About Nothing* and *The Novella*." *Shakespeare Yearbook*, 13 (2002), 419–441. Ranging widely over dramatic and nondramatic materials, Redmond explores the Elizabethan concept of Italy as background to the action of the play.

Shaw, George Bernard. *Shaw on Shakespeare*, ed. Edwin Wilson. London: Cassell, 1961. Pp. 135–151. Shaw delivers acerbic and witty reviews of the play and some productions.

Wells, Stanley. "Editorial treatment of foul-paper texts: *Much Ado About Nothing* as a test case." *Review of English Studies*, 31 (1980), 1–16. Though the notion of "foul-paper texts" has been well challenged in recent years, this is still a full, valuable account of problems and possibilities in the early printed text of the play.

Wynne-Davies, Marion, ed. *New Casebooks: Much Ado About Nothing and The Taming of the Shrew.* New York: Palgrave Press, 2001. This casebook reprints some superb articles—those of Harry Berger Jr. and Barbara Everett above, as well as S. P. Cerasano's discussion of Elizabethan women and slander and Penny Gay's account of feminism and recent productions.